Crisis In:
KOREA

YOSSEF BODANSKY

BOOKS

A Division Of Shapolsky Publishers

Crisis In: Korea

S.P.I. BOOKS
A division of Shapolsky Publishers, Inc.

ISBN 1-56171-332-5

For any additional information, contact:

S.P.I. BOOKS/Shapolsky Publishers, Inc.
136 West 22nd Street
New York, NY 10011
212/633-2022 / FAX 212/633-2123

Manufactured in Canada

10 9 8 7 6 5 4 3 2 1

CONTENTS

Introduction

BY CONGRESSMAN
BILL McCOLLUM

North Korea's unstable economic situation and impending power shift from Kim Il-Song to his son has the potential to start another war in that region. This time it's strongly believed that North Korea has the operational capability to hit key strategic objectives in its area of operation. In effect it could blast South Korea back into the stone age with nuclear weapons.

It's a chilling scenario but Yossef Bodansky, Director of the Republican Task Force on Terrorism and Unconventional Warfare, makes a convincing argument for it. Officially it's been difficult for America to point a finger at nuclear weapons stockpiled in North Korea's backyard, but Bodansky stacks clue upon clue for a picture that all too clearly points to this evidence.

As of early 1994 there is little doubt that North Korea possesses at least a few nuclear warheads with launch capabilities to hit key targets in its desired arena of control.

Defectors from North Korea give indications that their arsenal may be even larger than the current estimate of six weapons. One defector reported the existence of an underground nuclear plant in the northern region near the Chinese border. This location provides easy access to the roads and railroad coming out of Siberia which simplifies the transfer of nuclear material from Russia. A senior North Korean official tells of nuclear weapons hidden in an underground warehouse in the mountains outside the capital of Pyongyang.

A possible North Korean war plan might involve a preemptive launch of nuclear strikes against a few select objectives in South Korea and Japan, perhaps U.S. military bases in Japan. Indeed, Bodansky paints a dark picture of the pressures building in North Korea's economic and leadership structure that could lead to it taking on the U.S. through an attack on its allies.

Definitely not a scenario to make Americans sleep well at night.

After the fall of communism in the Soviet Union, most Americans felt that we no longer had dangerous enemies. We are learning that danger arises as easily from small nations with nuclear weapons as from large nations. It's the size of the weapon, not the size of the country that counts.

In this aftermath of the cold war, when so many nations have let down their guards *there is* need for continued vigilance and analysis of potential troublemakers.

I know of no finer expert at unraveling and explaining the behind the scenes maneuverings of North Korea than Yossef Bodansky. For more than five years, he has served as Director of the House Republican Task Force on Terrorism and Unconventional Warfare, of which I serve as chairman. His often controversial reports have proved to be prescient in predicting terrorist activities and threats against America and its Allies. The Task Force has been an independent voice in alerting the U.S. government to these threats. During this time, it has exposed numerous state-sponsored terrorist operations, including the counterfeiting of U.S. $100 bills by Iran and Syria.

This is why it is vital that all Americans read *Crisis In: Korea*. It's only by learning about our adversaries and educating our citizens that America can remain safe and protect its freedoms.

Bill McCollum (R-FL)
United States House of Representatives
Washington, D.C.

PREFACE

The Koreans call their country *Choson* which translates to "morning freshness." The formal translation of the country's name, Korea, is "The Land of the Morning Calm." How ironic that modern-day Korea is one of the hottest crisis spots in the world. Divided between the Democratic People's Republic of Korea (DPRK or North Korea) and the Republic of Korea (ROK or South Korea), this tense peninsula is on the verge of exploding into what could potentially become a global nuclear war.

North Korea is in the closing phase of a traumatic succession, in which power is being transferred from its near-dead founder and dictator Kim Il-Song (b. 1912), to his son, Kim Jong-Il (b. 1942). The succession takes place at a time when North Korea is on the verge of economic collapse due to the failed *Juche* communist doctrine. Adding pressure to the region is the relationship between the United States and South Korea. The fact that North Korea now has operational military nuclear capability, imperils not only its neighbors, South Korea and Japan but also the rest of the world.

North Korea is shaped in the image of Kim Il-Song. Under his rule the DPRK has become an instrument for the realization of what they believe to be their manifest destiny , the establishment of a regime in Korea unified by force, and based on their xenophobic interpretation of Marxism-Leninism called the *Juche* Doctrine. Through the ruthless implementation of *Juche*-based policies, North Korea has evolved into an aggressive military power, and, at the same time, an impoverished country on the brink of total economic collapse. It is in this abnormal situation that the key to the crisis lies.

Present-day North Korea is an unintended product of the Cold War, an instrument of the abandoned Soviet grand strategy. The Soviets established, armed and consolidated the Kim Il-Song regime in Pyongyang, and bankrolled the communist effort in the Korean War of 1950-53.

Understandably, Korea's tremendous strategic importance increased after events like the war in Vietnam and the collapse of the USSR.

Since the end of the Second World War, Moscow and Beijing have used the situation in Korea to measure the West's attitude toward communist countries. Any miscalculation by the USSR and the PRC could have led to a new Korean War and, in all likelihood, a nuclear Third World War.

Kim Il-Song eagerly supported the use of Korea in this way by the communist powers. In fact, he wanted his small backward state to become the most active and assertive pawn in the Cold War, and, in the process, achieve the unification of Korea by force of arms.

In retrospect, the communists were right about how useful Korea would be to them. During the Vietnam War, for example, Washington imposed self-restraint largely due to fear of Chinese becoming involved like they had in the war in Korea. At present, much of the US acquiescence to human rights abuses and questionable trade practices in China, is motivated by Washington's concern not to alienate Beijing, and thus lose influence in tumultuous Pyongyang.

Meanwhile, having convinced himself of his own crucial importance in the history of Marxist-Leninist world revolution, and faced with his own mortality and the collapse of the Soviet Union, Kim Il-Song and his son are now even more determined to live up to what they believe to be their responsibility. As a result, North Korea, once a tool of others expected to play only a supporting role, has taken the lead in the confrontation with the US-led West. The Kims are convinced that, irrespective of the horrendous consequences for North Korea itself, war is imperative for the restoration of a global communist revolutionary movement. The entire leadership in Pyongyang support this world view and are willing to pay the ultimate price for realizing this historical objective.

The transfer of power in Pyongyang from Kim Il-Song to Kim Jong-Il is nearly complete, as are their preparations for a major military strike. They see war as their opportunity to break out of a global ideological deadlock and a collapsing economy. The attack could be coordinated with Syria and Iran in the Middle East in order to overwhelm the US and the West.

While building their military, North Korea has, like China, begun economic relations with the West, thus maturing their grand strategy.

Kim Il-Song has cleverly integrated the aspirations of the military with the goals of the people. So much so that they are compelled to operate as a single bloc in support of the regime. The entire younger generation has been mobilized into active participation in the ascent of Kim Jong-Il.

North Korea's aggressive stance, in effect, issues the West an ultimatum: either bail out the North Korean economy and finance its industrial modernization or it will strike out, shattering the stability of the entire Pacific Rim. Indeed, a senior North Korean official acknowledged back in June 1992 that "North Korea may end up taking a certain type of military action for its survival if [the] superpowers support only one side."

North Korea is so small and their economy is so weak that their threats would have been ignored if not for the growing importance of the Pacific rim in world affairs and the global economy.

The Korean Peninsula is located in north-east Asia, off the northern coast of China and facing the southern islands of Japan. (see fig.1) It is rectangular in shape with an average width of about 150 miles, stretching less than 600 miles from the Chinese border to the Sea of Japan. The size of the entire peninsula is about 85,000 square miles (including 3,000 islands), about the same as the State of New York or Great Britain. Korea is characterized by mountainous terrain covered with thick woods and has a harsh winter climate. (see fig.2)

A major de stabilizing factor on the peninsula is the sharp difference between North Korea and South Korea, aside from politics. South Korea is only about three quarters the size of North Korea but has almost twice the people (over 44 million, according to a July 1992 census). The biggest difference between the two Koreas is economic. North Korea's GNP is $23.3b

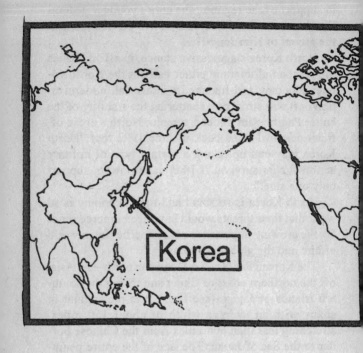

Fig. 1 — The strategic position of the Korean peninsula in the Pacific rim and in relation to the west coast of the United States

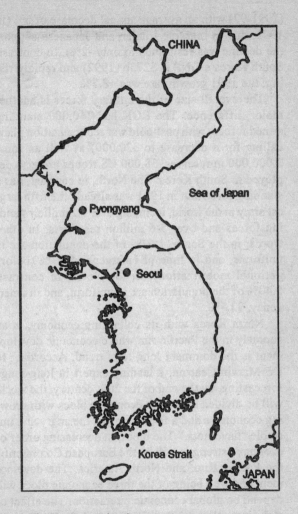

Fig. 2 — The Korean peninsula

(1991-92) with an average annual decrease of 5% (in 1992, due to massive Iranian and Japanese support the decline was restrained to only -2%). In contrast, South Korea's GNP is $273b (1992) and rapidly rising, the 1991 growth rate was +8.7%.

The overall size of the military forces is another major difference. The ROK has 740,000 standing armed forces (with post-cold war reorganization plans calling for a decrease to 320,000) as well as some 3,000,000 in reserves. 38,000 US troops are also deployed in South Korea. The North, in contrast, has a standing force that in 1991 was already the fifth largest army in the world, including over 1.2 million standing forces and over 5-6 million reservists. In other words, in the South, 1.67% of the population are in uniforms, and in time of emergency 8.47% (before national mobilization). In the North, in contrast, 5.40% of the population are in uniform, and in emergency, 32.4%.

North Korea with its collapsing economy, is an anomaly in the Pacific rim where economic development is the dominant long-term trend. According to Dr. Marvin Ceatron, a leading expert in long-range forecasting, by the end of the 20th century, the world will be divided into three economic blocs with growing economies and a fourth bloc of the angry and unstable "have-nots." The blocs, in decreasing order of economic strength, will be the European Community, the Pacific Rim, and North America. The development and well being of the three economic blocs will depend on global economic interaction. The effect of stability within the Pacific rim nations will continue to increase in importance for both the region and the entire world.

Therefore, the impact of a major disruption by North Korea will reverberate throughout the entire developed world, way beyond the area directly affected by military action.

North Korea is on the verge of starvation and only unification with the South can conceivably save it from a total economic collapse. Dr. Ceatron believes that the border between North and South Korea will disappear soon after the death of Kim Il-Song. The question is, what kind of unification will take place?

One option is for the South to willingly absorb the North. This option is presently not favored by Seoul, fearing a repeat of the crises in Germany following its unification. The other option, frighteningly more likely, is that the North will swallow the South by force of arms, destroying its economic infrastructure and wealth in the process.

The Pacific rim is particularly important to the United States. The European Community is increasingly looking into Eastern Europe as the primary venue for its economic development and expansion. For the United States, beyond North America, further development of the American economy lies in the Pacific Rim.

Although the future of the Pacific rim is bright, the region is still unstable. China is still wavering between cooperation and confrontation with the West. Like North Korea, China has also been building its military. Furthermore, it has failed to modernize its huge economy and infrastructure to meet the challenges of the future. Meanwhile, Japan is still in recession. South Korea and Taiwan are the two real dynamic players. Their progress will have a direct impact on the extent of the US share in the economic development of the entire Pacific rim.

It is in this context that Korea is more important than ever before. It is a bridge between China and Japan, whose interaction is the key to long-term economic recovery and expansion. Korea also provides unique access for the US not only to the Pacific rim states, but even to Siberia (once Russia recovers). The Korean Peninsula is vitally important to the whole world.

The rapidly escalating crisis in Korea threatens everyone. It is therefore essential to understand how North Korea developed its strategy and built its armed forces to the point of posing a nuclear threat to the entire world.

Crisis in Korea is divided into four parts that cover the key aspects needed to understand the current crisis:

The first part surveys the unique history of the Korean Peninsula till the end of the Korean War. Emphasis is put on the establishment of North Korea, the rise of Kim Il-Song, the establishment of Soviet control, and the role of the Korean War (1950-53).

The second part covers the rise of North Korean military. Special attention is paid to the development of their concept of war, the massive military build-up, the development of its chemical and nuclear weapons and concludes with a detailed description of the type of war they would prefer to wage against South Korea and the American forces.

The third and fourth parts deal with how the current succession crisis in Pyongyang, the transfer of power from Kim Il-Song to Kim Jong-Il, affects their willingness to start a potentially nuclear war.

The book concludes with an assessment of the possible course of a new Korean War and the viable options for the United States.

The opinions expressed in this book are mine, and do not necessarily reflect the views of all the members of the House Republican Task Force on Terrorism and Unconventional Warfare, US Congress, or any other branch of the US Government.

Yossef Bodansky
Washington DC.
April 1994

PART I

ROOTS OF CONFLICT

The history of the Korean Peninsula is dominated by two trends:

First, although Koreans yearn for a unified state, rivalries within the ruling elites often resulted in separation and internal strife.

Second, because of the strength of its mighty neighbors China, Japan, and Russia, Korean rulers have repeatedly tried to ally themselves with one of them for protection.

Consequently, Korea has been a center of regional dynamics and power struggles from the beginnings of its history to this day.

1

ROOTS

Koreans are an ancient and homogenous people. Their ancestors migrated from Central Asia and Manchuria over five thousand years ago. From that time until the present, the population has remained essentially unchanged.

The Korean Peninsula is one of the earliest places inhabited by an organized group, first settled by permanent communities around 3000 BC. The first Kingdom of Choson was established around 2333 BC. by the legendary King Tangun who, tradition has it, was of "divine origin." However, the country could not hold together and, within a few hundred years, the Korean kingdom gradually disintegrated into the "Three Kingdoms" of Paekche (southwestern Korea), Koguryo (northern Korea), and Silla (southeastern Korea). At first, the line dividing the peninsula from the mainland was vague and any sense of statehood was lacking. Unity spread among the three kingdoms, which became strong socio-economic centers.

A very important event in the history of ancient

Korea was the arrival of Saje Kija, a Chinese scholar and holyman, in 1122 BC., along with 5,000 of his Chinese followers. The Chinese brought their traditions of organized government, written history, and other facets of advanced culture unknown to the Koreans. Over the next few hundreds years the Chinese would significantly affect the establishment of modern Korea. However, Korea kept their own roots. The ability to absorb foreign influences while preserving Korean uniqueness saved them from being swallowed up by their stronger neighbors.

By the first century BC. there was a growing flow of Chinese migrants into Korea. Chinese military forces frequently traveled with them for their protection. The Chinese immigrants established agricultural communities in the northern parts of the peninsula and, by 108 BC., there were four major, well-organized Chinese colonies in the north. Gradually, Korea became a Chinese protectorate. The effects of Chinese culture can still be felt, but at no time was Korea's own culture overwhelmed.

Eventually the Chinese influence waned, and around 300 AD. the "Three Kingdoms" reemerged, this time as independent political entities. Over the next few hundred years, the three kingdoms fought amongst themselves to unify under a single leader and in the process developed a very sophisticated civilization.

During this period the Silla Kingdom rose to prominence and unified the peninsula under King Kyongdok who ruled from 742 to 764, making significant contributions to Korean political culture. The active assistance received from the Chinese was instrumental to the first Silla Kings' success in pacifying the northern parts of the peninsula.

Korea embarked on their first dedicated construction projects and their economy was strengthened through diverse and large scale trading with China. As a sign of its new stature, Korea was recognized as an independent state by China in 735.

Silla rulers developed a highly centralized state government which controlled all economic and religious activities. Ruling for over a thousand years, the Silla Dynasty left imprints that still shape Korea today.

At the beginning of the 10th century, internal strife and factionalism began showing in the highest levels of the Silla elite. It did not take long for rebel forces to seize the opportunity and in 935 General Wang Kon (known as King Taejo after his death) forced the last Silla king to abdicate. A Koryo Dynasty was soon established in Kaesong, and immediately sought to accelerate economic development.

Korea expanded its political contacts, economic relations, and cultural ties with China. Chinese influence was enhanced after the Manchurian invasion of 1011 which exposed Korea to a new flow of Chinese migrants and officials. In 1044, in order to defend Korea from further raids by Manchurian marauders, Koryo built a stone wall across the peninsula just south of the Yalu river.

The Koryo Dynasty was drawn into the Far East's power struggles with the Mongols. Mongol armies invaded the peninsula in 1231 and swiftly overwhelmed the Koryo kingdom. The Mongols wrought major destruction on Korean culture and civilization, burning most of their ancient writings, written on wooden blocks. Not long afterwards, however, the Mongols established a friendly administration in Korea, officially still run by the Koryo, and won the cooperation of several local rulers. These rulers were close allies of Chinese-Mongol Emperor Kublai Khan, and Korea benefited tremendously from the absorption of Mongol concepts of modern government.

But such close cooperation with Beijing had a price. The Koreans would help the Mongols in several regional military projects, most notably in the building of military fleets and the consequent disastrous attempts to invade Japan in 1274 and again in 1281.

The most important legacy of the Mongol-Koryo era was the rise of the military elite as the major political power in Korea. Senior military commanders were recognized more than ever before as key political figures in all aspects of government. It was not long before a fiercely nationalist military elite would take back power on behalf of the Korean people. In the mid-14th century, several Korean senior officers led by General Yi Song-Gye began a revolt against the Chinese. The turning point was in 1364 when they finally defeated the main Chinese force. The armed struggle continued for another generation before General Yi was able to consolidate his rule over Korea.

In 1392 General Yi Song-Gye overthrew the Koryo dynasty, proclaimed himself King, and established the Yi Dynasty that would rule Korea (now known as the Kingdom of Choson) until the early 20th century. King Yi knew Korea needed a regional alliance and chose the Ming Dynasty in China. Again Korea was exposed to Chinese influence. Confucianism, for example, replaced the Buddhism that established itself in Korea during Silla rule. Chinese culture and practices came to dominate Korean social life. There was a flourishing in science, technology, arts, and culture, integrating indigenous Korean roots with Chinese influence.

Korean identity was developing. King Sejong (who ruled from 1418 to 1450) conquered the areas north of the wall and built forts to protect the Korean communities. These conquests, though small in scale, greatly determined the boundaries of modern Korea.

Korea turned inward. In 1446 King Sejong sponsored a phonetic alphabet for Korea with only 28 characters, called *Hunmin chongum* meaning "correct sounds for people." Popularly known as *Hangul*, this alphabet is so logically arranged that it can be mastered within a few hours. The *Hangul* and its ease of learning was the key to a massive literacy campaign throughout the country. This high level of literacy prevails today in the Korean countryside, a unique situation in Asia, especially the Far East.

Several hundred years of peace and prosperity followed under the Chinese "umbrella," resulting in the rapid development and enrichment of Korea. Little wonder the Yi elite accumulated massive fortunes. It was not long before they became lazy and corrupt.

By the late 16th century a power struggle between the region's giants was emerging. Japanese rulers saw the Korean Peninsula as the most vulnerable access point into mainland China. Consequently, between 1592 and 1598, the Japanese repeatedly invaded the Asian mainland through Korea. Although the Japanese invasions largely failed, the danger was obvious to the Chinese leaders. In the early 17th century, once the Manchu Dynasty consolidated its internal power,

China devoted its attention to strengthening its hold over Korea. Chinese armies invaded Korea repeatedly between 1627 and 1637, but failed to gain anything substantial before being distracted by power struggles for Beijing.

Once the dust settled, Korea withdrew into self-imposed xenophobic isolation. In 1638 the country was closed to foreigners with a mandatory death sentence for violators. Korea soon became known as the "Hermit Kingdom." But because of its common heritage with China and inseparable economic relations, the Chinese influence nevertheless remained strong.

Korea's isolation continued until 1876, when the Japanese forced it to grant them access into certain ports for commercial purposes. It did not take Japan long to use the limited Korean concessions to force their way in and expand their influence on Korea.

Meanwhile, Western powers were increasing their presence in northeast Asia. Korea could no longer remain in isolation. Within a few years, additional treaties, comparable to the one with Japan, were signed with other foreign powers. The United States was the first Western power to gain access to Korean ports in 1882. A year later, with the encouragement of China, Korea signed a treaty of friendship with the United States. China's reasons were obvious. It sought to balance the growing Japanese influence which it could not resist on its own. Indeed Korea signed, in quick succession, trade agreements with Russia and various European powers. By 1886, Korea had signed comprehensive agreements and access treaties with virtually all the world powers that had interests in the Far East. Korea's isolation was over.

By the late 19th century, an intense international

struggle began for the domination, and ultimately control, of the Korea. It's strategic location was obvious.

Despite the opening of Korea to the West and to Russia, Japanese influence remained pervasive, if not outright dominant. In the second half of the 19th century, the Japanese were very active in weakening the Yi Dynasty. The Japanese provoked internal dissent and even actively assisted various factions (with weapons, funds, propaganda, and expertise) to rebel against the central authorities. These revolts gradually escalated and spread all over the country.

Rebellion and violence spread into the northern part of Korea, where there were concentrations of Chinese. Beijing could not avoid reacting. The first major clash between Chinese and Japanese armed forces on the Korean Peninsula took place in 1884.

China realized the gravity of the Japanese threat and was determined to contain it. In 1894-95, the Chinese again intervened. Under the pretext of answering Korea's plea for help, Chinese armies invaded and battled Japanese forces entirely on Korean soil. The Chinese were soundly defeated, and the Japanese took full control over Korea, including even its internal affairs.

The rise of the Japanese Empire in Korea alarmed Russia, and Russian forces increased their presence in northeast Asia, including Manchuria. In October 1895, Japanese troops killed Korea's Queen Min, captured King Kojong, and killed or arrested the entire royal family, all in an effort to impose a Japanese-dominated regime. But the Yis remained defiant and in 1896 King Kojong fled to the Russian representatives in Seoul. There, in the name of Korea, he appealed to Russia for help and protection. Russian troops were sent to Korea to balance the Japanese presence.

The Russian effort failed to reverse the surge of Japanese might. Japan made an offer to Russia to divide the peninsula along the 38th parallel into zones of influence. Russia refused and, instead, intensified its strategic penetration into Manchuria as a means to bolster its hold over Korea and the region. In 1898, the Russians gained strategic Port Arthur on the Pacific coast. But most alarming to Tokyo was Russia's dispatching of 150,000 troops, via Korea and Manchuria, to fight in the Boxer Rebellion in China in 1900-1901. Moreover, most of these Russian troops were eventually withdrawn to Korea instead of Russia. To add further insult, Russia completed the Trans-Siberian Railway in 1903, enabling them to rapidly transport men and material to Korea from Central Asia, and even from as far away as European Russia.

Tokyo saw direct confrontation with Russia as inevitable. In February 1904, the Japanese fleet attacked the Russian army in Port Arthur, starting the 1904-1905 Russo-Japanese War. Japan was fighting Russia, in essence, for the future control of northeast Asia (Manchuria and Korea). In the battles that followed, Russia suffered serious defeats. It lost its entire fleet, and the islands along the Siberian coast and north of Japan. A triumphant Japan forced King Kojong of Korea to abdicate in July 1907. Then, in August 1910, Japan officially annexed Korea and established a military government in Seoul. Korea would remain a Japanese colony until 1945.

2

THE ROAD TO MODERN KOREA

Despite the tight control of the Japanese, the two cultures were not completely alien to one another and Korea continued to develop internally during the 1920s and 1930s.

Tokyo was determined to fully exploit the human and industrial potential of Korea to support its military drives over the rest of Asia. As a result, Koreans were provided with higher technical education. It was a prelude to widespread industrialization.

The price of Japanese rule was harsh repression but ultimately, the Japanese were responsible for modernizing Korea and laying the foundations of South Korea's current economic might. The Japanese built a massive network of good roads, ports and airports, as well as electrical wiring. They modernized the agriculture base so fewer people could produce more food, freeing peasants for labor gangs to man the massive works programs. As well, the consolidation of

Japanese control over Manchuria gave unprecedented mobility throughout northeast Asia which resulted in many modern day commercial relationships for Korea.

Though heavily repressed, the people of Korea consistently rebelled against the Japanese. Resistance had begun in 1910, virtually the moment the Japanese gained their hold over the country. A major protest in March 1919 turned into an armed uprising. Members of the urban elite (students, teachers, etc.) were protesting the Japanization of the education system and Korean cultural life. The protests spread so rapidly that they escalated out of control and, by the time they were suppressed, up to 2 million people had become involved. Numerous armed clashes by this time were breaking out all over Korea. Some 7,000 Koreans were killed, tens of thousands arrested, and hundreds executed.

Although the uprisings were short-lived and futile, they gave birth to the opposition movements that ultimately shaped modern Korea. By the 1920s, two types of Korean opposition and resistance movements emerged: nationalist (conservative and traditionalist); and communist (internationalist).

The Korean Communist movement ruling North Korea today is a product of both nationalist sentiment and the politics of northeast Asia. Soon after the 1917 revolution, Soviet Russia embarked on a drive to incite communist revolution in China and the Far East. They trained local revolutionary groups and provided military assistance.

The militant communist movement in Korea is a by-product of the failure of the first Soviet attempts to launch revolutions in China. After the collapse of the communist uprising in Shanghai and Canton in the late 1920s, and the consolidation of the National-ist regime in China, Moscow moved the center of com-munist subversion to Manchuria because of its prox-imity to the Soviet Union. Koreans actively joined the Soviet ranks from the beginning, and quickly rose to senior command positions. Thus, Chinese and Korean communist guerrillas fought against the Japanese in northeast China in the early 1930s.

The North-East Anti-Japanese United Army was the most important communist force fighting Japan between 1936 and 1941. Of 46 senior commanders and political officers in this Army, eight were Kore-ans.

One of the most important strategists waging guer-rilla warfare in China was the legendary Yang Jingyu (Chinese). Yang Jingyu would die in battle in late Feb-ruary 1940, after a lengthy pursuit by Japanese spe-cial forces. One of Yang Jingyu's proteges was a young Korean revolutionary named Kim Song-Ju. He es-caped to Manchuria after participating in a revolu-tionary communist group in his high school for which he was expelled, and arrested. In Manchuria Kim Song-Ju joined the Communist partisans, and assumed the *nom de guerre* Kim Il-Song, which means One Star. He soon became the protege of a political officer in the 2nd Directional Army (a part of the North-East Anti-Japanese United Army), Wei Zhengmin (Chi-nese). Wei Zhengmin would be killed in combat in early March 1941, during one of the last actions of the guerrilla army.

Meanwhile, by the mid 1930s Kim Il-Song was ris-ing from the ranks to become the commander of the 6th Division of the 2nd Directional Army of the 1st

Route Army. Communist guerrilla forces at that time were fighting against the Japanese occupation and local Manchuko forces, as well as against rich local Chinese farmers and warlords who led their own private armies. Despite the great sacrifices made by the guerrillas, their efforts were considered merely harassment by the Japanese, not a serious strategic threat.

The Manchurian-Korean guerrilla forces continued to fight until 1941 when Japanese pressure forced them to cut back their activities to a bare minimum. In the aftermath of the fierce battle in March 1941 where Wei Zhengmin was killed, many of the guerrilla leaders withdrew to the safety of the Soviet Far East. Kim Il-Song led a whole group of senior and mid-rank Korean commanders across the border.

The Korean guerrillas crossed into the Soviet Union at a very peculiar time because at the time the Soviet secret police were uncertain about the loyalties of the Korean population in the Soviet provinces. After all, Korea was a Japanese colony and the Japanese army drew its supplies and reinforcements from Korea. Therefore, large segments of the Soviet Union's own Korean population were exiled by Stalin to Kazakhstan and Uzbekistan in Central Asia.

The Korean communist fighters who had arrived in the USSR in 1941 were completely dedicated to the communist cause and fiercely loyal to Moscow. After putting them at first under the command of the Chinese, the Soviet Union decided to use them as the core of a Soviet-controlled Korean Army. The most promising among them were sent to higher military schools, primarily the Okeanskaya Field School near Vladivostok, the Voroshilov Camp near Nikolsk, and a field training site in Khabarovsk. There, they were groomed to play a future role in a Soviet dominated Korea, present-day North Korea. Kim Il-Song's wife followed him to the USSR and they had a son, Kim Jong-Il. As a child Kim Jong-Il was known by the Russian name Yura.

Once Moscow committed itself to participating in World War II in the Far East (the USSR remained neutral until August 1945), additional Soviet-Koreans were recruited to join Moscow's Korean Army. The Korean unit was an integral part of the Soviet Armed Forces. Kim Il-Song returned to Korea after the Japanese surrender and the Soviet occupation of the north.

Meanwhile, in the southern part of Korea, things were different. Some of the opposition leaders emigrated to the U.S to escape Japanese control. Others who had been exiled to China became increasingly involved in anti-Japanese terrorism.

South Korean nationalists sought alliance with the U.S. because they considered it the strategic rival of Japan and the only power capable of bringing about their freedom.

Thus, by the 1940s, the Northern and Southern anti-Japanese Koreans were divided between two ideologically opposed elites. The polarization of the two increased during World War II. In November 1943, at the Cairo Summit, the allies agreed that post-War Korea should be "free and independent." In the Potsdam Summit, in July 1945, the allies agreed further on the 38th parallel as the demarcation line of their zones of influence on the Korean Peninsula. The roots of the current crisis were sown.

3

ENTER THE COMMUNIST FACTOR

The consolidation of communist rule in North Korea under the leadership of Kim Il-Song, the victory of the Chinese communists in China in 1948-49, and the Korean War in 1950-53, were all part of a strategic transformation of East Asia.

At present, in 1994, the situation in East Asia is explosive because the local forces created by Moscow during these transformations are no longer controlled by post-USSR Moscow.

Although the Soviet Union and Japan fought a fierce border war in Khalkin Gol [Nomonhan] on the Mongolia-Manchuria border in the fall of 1939, the USSR remained neutral during most of World War II. Instead, despite intense mistrust between Stalin and Mao Zedong, the USSR provided tremendous amounts of military aid to the Chinese communist forces that were fighting the Japanese. With tremendous amounts of Western assistance flowing to the Soviet Union, and with Moscow's need for Western recognition of its power in Eastern Europe, Stalin realized that he would have to join the allies in the war against Japan. Therefore, in 1943, and formally in 1945, the Soviet Union agreed to join the other allies in the war against Japan only after the complete defeat of Germany.

Although the Soviet Union was officially neutral in the Far East during most of World War II, it was very active in preparing for the postwar world. Its primary objective was the expansion of the communist sphere of influence.

A most important aspect of this effort was the establishment of a network of loyal groups that, once the war was over, would rise up and seize power in their areas, establishing Communist regimes, loyal and subservient to the Soviet Union. Korea was crucial in this grand design. Korea could serve as a uniquely effective basis for leaping into postwar Japan. Specifically, the Korean community in Japan could be quickly mobilized from a base in Korea. (Indeed, the Japanese-Korean community is still extremely loyal to Pyongyang rather than Seoul.) Similarly, the Chinese communists had their own legitimate and indigenous communist leadership under Mao whom Stalin mistrusted but needed. A Soviet-dominated Korea provided the USSR with crucial alternative access to the Pacific coast in case tension with the Chinese increased or China's Nationalist forces defeated Mao's Communist revolution.

Indeed, during the 1940s, Moscow prepared to take over Korea the moment World War II ended. Within the safety of the USSR the Soviets formed a Korean Government consisting of Soviet-Korean military, security and party bureaucracy, to be installed by the

Soviet Armed Forces after the war.

The Soviets also organized a web of groups inside Korea for local leaderships that would legitimize the Soviet-installed government in the eyes of the Korean population. During the war, these local groups were organized as "People's Committees" throughout the Korean Peninsula. They were provided modest, though important, political and military support during World War II. They would indeed prove a strategic asset immediately after the war.

The USSR attacked Japan in the summer of 1945 conducting a succession of deep offensives. They consider their Manchurian Campaign, lasting from 9 August to 2 September 1945, to be one of the most significant operations in the war. "This truly lightning-fast campaign lasted just 24 days. But in terms of scope, dynamic quality, and final results it is one of the most important campaigns of World War II," stressed Marshal SU M. Zakharov.

To a great degree, the current Russian concept of winning total victory in a non-nuclear initial period of war is based on the experience and lessons of the Manchurian Campaign. Gen. S.P. Ivanov stressed that "The campaign of the Soviet forces in the Far East constituted a profound contribution to the development of the Soviet Art of War, primarily in the art of preparation, and the delivery of initial crushing strikes on the enemy in the outbreak of the war." The Soviet campaign in the Far East was a classic example of the art of strategic leadership. The Manchurian Campaign was indeed unparalleled during World War II. The offensive was conducted on a 5,000-km wide front with depths of 600 to 800km. In 25 days, the Soviet Armed Forces smashed the Japanese Kwantung Army, capturing most of its equipment.

The Soviet Union considered World War II a major opportunity for communist control of the Far East. The defeat of Japan signified the defeat of their only real opposition in the region.

The Soviet control over southern Sakhalin and the Kuril Islands was recognized by the Western Allies. The US accepted the Soviet occupation of Manchuria and Korea north of the 38th Parallel, and recognized these territories as Soviet areas of influence. The Soviets considered their victory in the Manchurian Campaign as the decisive element in the eventual rise to power of the Chinese Communist Party. They perceived their only failure to be not having taken control of Hokkaido Island after the Japanese surrender. (Had the allies invaded Japan, the USSR would have been responsible for the occupation of Hokkaido.)

A study of Sino-Soviet relations by Soviet experts O.B. Borisov and B.T. Kolosov emphasized the strategic importance of the Manchurian Campaign. "The defeat of the crack Kwantung Army in 1945 by Soviet troops supported by armed forces of the Mongolian People's Republic and the People's Liberation Army of China (PLA) played a decisive role in the defeat of militaristic Japan, and in the complete expulsion of the Japanese occupiers from Chinese soil, and was, as well, the most important international factor in the victory of the Chinese revolution. Manchuria, liberated by Soviet troops, became a dependable military and strategic base of operations for Chinese revolutionary forces. It was from this base that Chinese Communists led the people in the decisive struggle against the corrupt Kuomintang regime."

After the war in the Far East, the Soviets sought

to annex only territories which they considered to be critical to their security. Confronted with the growing U.S. military power in the Pacific, the Soviets annexed southern Sakhalin and the Kuril Islands, not just as a historical vindication, as Stalin emphasized, but also in order to block Western naval access to the Sea of Okhotsk.

In Manchuria, the USSR launched the steady buildup of military support for the Chinese Communist Party, equipping them with first-class weapons that had been taken as booty from the Kwantung Army, including: 4,300 guns, mortars and grenade launchers, 686 tanks, 861 aircraft, 2,321 trucks, over 13,000 machine guns, and huge quantities of ammunition including entire factories for their manufacture.

The Soviet Union established The High Command of Troops of the Far East on 22 May 1947 with Headquarters in Khabarovsk. The Soviets channeled their military assistance to the Chinese communists through this command. Later, following the outbreak of the Korean War, the Soviet mobilization and the deployment of Soviet military personnel into Korea was also conducted from this center of Far East operations. Following Stalin's death and the progress in the negotiations for an armistice in Korea, the High Command of Troops of the Far East was abolished.

4

THE ESTABLISHMENT OF NORTH KOREA

When the Soviet forces entered Korea in August-September 1945, there were actually two armies marching in parallel. Prominent was the liberating Soviet Army, under the command of Gen. Ivan M. Chistiakov. He entered Pyongyang as commander of the 25th Division, and became the commander of the Soviet forces in Korea. The second army, of much smaller scale, was led by Gen. Maj. Nikolai Lebedev, ostensibly Chistiakov's Chief Executive Officer. Lebedev's army was in Korea to transform the country into a Soviet satellite, and to install Moscow's Koreans at the helm.

The ultimate priority of the Soviet forces in North Korea was to prepare for expansion. This is evident from the identity of the two senior "civilian/political" advisers deployed in 1946 to Pyongyang. Both were veteran intelligence officers. The first, Gerasim M. Balasanov, had experience in Japan, and spoke fluent

Japanese but little Korean. The second, Anatoliy I.
Shabshin, served in Seoul as deputy consul where his
responsibilities included maintaining contacts with the
communist underground. His knowledge and expertise was South Korea.

Meanwhile, during the World War II, Kim Il-Song
was commissioned Captain and later Major in the 88th
Brigade of the Soviet Armed Forces. Although the
25th Division liberated Pyongyong on August 27th,
the 88th Brigade under the command of Lebedev did
not enter Korea until September 19th, when Soviet
rule was secure.

Kim Il-Song brought with him some 40 loyalists,
all in Soviet uniforms, who would staff his Headquarters in Pyongyang. From the very beginning, Kim Il-
Song "was created, cultivated and exists" solely based
on the decision of Moscow. "We created Kim Il-Song
from scratch, virtually," recalls Leonid Vanin who
served with Army Intelligence in Pyongyang at the
time. Indeed, Kim Il-Song's return to Pyongyang was
secured by a Soviet SMERSH (Special Forces) de-
tachment, as was his subsequent stay in his own capital. Under Lebedev, Soviet intelligence created and
consolidated Kim Il-Song as a political figure, tightly
controlling and navigating his course of action, including writing his speeches. Thus, Vanin concludes,
Kim Il-Song is "a simple and obedient border-crosser
who came within the sights of our intelligence authorities. More precisely, he was obliging, far from having
any ideas of his own, and capable of repeating what
was suggested to him."

Within a few days of his return to Pyongyang, Kim
Il-Song began visiting local communist leaders, especially the elders, in order to gain their support for the

Korean military government he claimed to be establishing. In effect, he sought their recognition, which he did not receive. Nevertheless, on 14 October 1945, the Soviets introduced the "Korean leaders" to the public in a major public rally in Pyongyang. The ceremony was attended by the entire Soviet High Command in Korea. Among the keynote speakers was the young Kim Il-Song, now in civilian clothes. He delivered a speech written for him by Soviet intelligence.

The Soviets moved carefully in establishing their proteges as leaders. At first, the Korean ruling elite were the leaders of the People's committees and other long-term communists who had stayed in Korea, enduring the war and Japanese repression with the public. The returning Soviet Koreans were kept in the shadows. In the meantime, the Soviets manipulated the government organizations from within, accumulating institutional power without openly challenging the older leaders.

By late 1946, the Soviets felt that their position was sufficiently secure to run "elections" and transfer power to their Koreans. This move led to the establishment of a full fledged Marxist-Leninist regime in Pyongyang. From 1946 to 47 in the aftermath of the elections, the Soviets and their Koreans purged the elite from remnants of any leftist organization not completely loyal to Kim Il-Song. A few "united fronts" and propaganda organizations were allowed to remain in order to create the image of an independent Pyongyang.

Once secure, the Soviets led Kim Il-Song in a ruthless purge of the communist elite itself. He established a joint leadership made up of "Partisans" (Koreans who fought in Manchuria and were later trained and prepared by the Soviets during the war) and "Soviet-Koreans" (Soviet-born Koreans who were ultimately integrated into the Pyongyang elite). These groups (and their children) still constitute the hard core of power in Pyongyang.

Then, Kim Il-Song, with Soviet assistance, launched an all-out personality cult campaign to legitimize his tight grip on power. He established himself as the "legendary guerrilla hero" whose feats against the Japanese, even if in Manchuria, ultimately facilitated the liberation of North Korea. This was the beginning of the current unprecedented personality cult that made Kim Il-Song a demi-god to his people. In the early 1990s, this campaign still persists.

In reality, Kim Il-Song had been an internationalist communist fighter, fighting first as part of a Chinese revolutionary army and then as part of the Soviet Armed Forces for the Marxist-Leninist Revolution.

5

THE MAKING OF PYONGYANG

There were three main phases in the Sovietization of North Korea:

The first phase lasted between August 1945 and January 1946. It was characterized by the genuine cooperation of the local Korean elite with the Soviets. The Korean leaders were organized into Interim People's Committees, made up primarily of communists and leftist-nationalists who had stayed behind and established a genuine following. These leaders were cooperating with Soviet representatives to build a communist regime in Pyongyang. Kim Il-Song and the Soviet-Koreans were not a part of this political elite. During this period, the Soviets manipulated and pushed the coalition members and their Interim People's Committees into self-destruction. Consequently, the Soviets created a vacuum at the top that their Koreans could now fill. The nationalist leaders themselves would be arrested and executed on the eve of the Korean War.

The second phase lasted between February 1946 and early 1948. It was yet another period where the Soviet-dominated regime still had to conceal itself within a "bogus coalition" so as not to alienate the North Korean population. This phase was in effect a more subtle, yet drastic, purge of the Korean communist leadership in order to make way for the rise of the USSR's own Koreans. Purges of the old Korean Communist Party were critical because these communists had been influenced by West European communism and they considered the center of Korea to be in the South.

As a replacement for the Interim People's Committees, the Soviets established the North Korean Provisional People's Committee in February 1946. The Committee was a so-called wider coalition, but was clearly dominated by Moscow's people and led by Kim Il-Song. The new Committee was devoted to "democratic reforms" and urged the widest possible array of political parties to join in a coalition. However, in reality, it was an instrument of the Soviet secret services for identifying competition and quietly purging them before they could hurt Moscow's interests.

Meanwhile, Kim Il-Song and his Partisans were emerging as the genuine Korean patriotic leadership. The Soviet-Koreans, still operating in the shadows, were gaining control over the administration and beaurocracy. The Partisans were then nominated to key positions of security. Also, in the name of building national armed forces, the Soviets and their allies oversaw the destruction of remnants of the military and guerrilla forces.

In July 1946, Kim Il-Song established the Workers' Party, on Soviet adviser Ignatov's orders, as a coalition of the North Korean Communist Party, detached from the Seoul-centered veteran Korean Communist Party. Kim Tu-Bong, a veteran partisan and old political hand, was "elected" Chairman of the WPK. Kim Il-Song was just the vice-chairman. This position, however, gave him greater freedom to operate and consolidate power, while Kim Tu-Bong and his followers took the blame for the purges. In these maneuvers Kim Il-Song proved himself as the best and most capable agent of the Soviet Union in Pyongyang.

The third phase of Sovietization lasted from February to September 1948, when the independence of the Democratic People's Republic of Korea (DPRK) was declared in North Korea. It constituted the consolidation of the Kim Il-Song regime in Pyongyang in a way that would ensure the strategic interests of Moscow. It was made abundantly clear that Kim Il-Song was the true power behind the leadership in Pyongyang. In early 1948, Kim Il-Song and the Soviet-Koreans led and accomplished yet another massive purge of the communist leadership. They got rid of all the veterans and nationalists who accepted Moscow's rule but were not wholly committed to Moscow.

It was clear that Kim Tu-Bong and the few veterans with him were merely titular heads, essentially in a powerless position. Kim Il-Song's candidates for positions at the Party's leadership were all accepted without challenge, while all other candidates were rejected. By the time the independence of North Korea was declared in September 1948 and Soviet forces withdrawn in December 1948, there was no longer any challenge to Kim Il-Song. He became the head of government with his loyalists safely entrenched in all ministerial and top positions.

Moscow was already confident back in February 1948 that Kim Il-Song was solidly in power. The ensuing purges served only to solidify his power base for the long term. Consequently, the withdrawal of most of the Soviet Armed Forces was completed quickly. A large group of Soviet advisers remained behind, as did virtually all their military equipment, from bases and airports, to aircraft and tanks, to stockpiles of ammunition and clothes. The equipment, for the new North Korean Army, would be organized by the Soviet advisors.

The establishment of communist military and security forces in North Korea had been one of the top priorities of the Soviet Union and its allies from the very beginning. In November 1945, the Soviets established a military ideological school for Korean officers so that by the time the first class graduated in 1947-48, they were totally loyal to Kim Il-Song and were ready to contribute to the consolidation of his power.

The Soviets also established a highly professional army largely trained in the USSR but integrating Manchurians loyal to Moscow and also local ideologically motivated rebels, resulting in a military machine effective in suppressing local revolts as well as launching an attack on the South.

The Soviets were thinking in the long term. Toward this end, several training centers for junior officers and NCOs were established in 1945. In 1946, the schools graduated the first classes in sufficient numbers to run a 20,000-troop army. Such a force soon transferred into Kim Il-Song's praetorian guard, which included personal guards, artillery and armored units, railway troops for transportation, construction troops for government facilities, and soldiers for secret police units. A school for Central Security Officers graduated the first class in 1947, thus laying the foundations for the political military elite.

The Korean People's Army (KPA) was formally established on 8 February 1948, seven months before the independence of North Korea. By then, the Russians had established basic military industries in Korea. The first machine guns, a copy of the Soviet World War II PPSh (M-41), were produced in 1948. Production of basic ammunition soon followed, as well as light artillery and other military products. Also, in 1948, after a few abortive starts, the KPA opened a new school for training officers and organizers for guerrilla and special operations in the south. The declared objective of the graduates was the subversion of the South. The main school was in Hoeryong, Hamyong Pukto, and became known as the Hoeryong Cadres School. It should be emphasized that the first school commander was O Chin-U, one of the Partisans perceived closest to Kim Il-Song and currently the DPRK's Minister of Defense.

Other North Korean military resources include Korean communist forces who fought in China throughout World War II and the Civil War. At the peak of the fighting, the Chinese Marshal Lin Biao had some 145,000 Koreans under his command. Their vital contribution to his forces would influence the PRC's involvement in the Korean War. The Korean troops in Manchuria were well organized and disciplined, and could significantly increase the conventional capabilities of the North Korean forces. In 1949-

50, some 100,000 of these Koreans, along with their weapons and equipment, crossed back into North Korea from Manchuria, and were quickly integrated into the fledgling North Korean Army in preparation for the major war.

Thus, in the spring of 1950, just before the final preparations for the Korean War were to be undertaken, the KPA was already about 120,000-135,000 troops strong. Its units were well organized and competently led. Each unit had a sizable core of combat veterans from World War II and the Chinese Civil War to provide leadership and example. Their heavy weapons included some 150 T-34 tanks and numerous 122mm towed artillery pieces, then among the most powerful and accurate in the world.

6

THE ESTABLISHMENT AND SUBVERSION OF SOUTH KOREA

On 6 September 1945, immediately after the surrender of Japan, a Korean "government" claiming to represent the People's Committees was established in Seoul virtually overnight and before the US/UK allied forces reached the country. It was a blatant, if ultimately futile, attempt to dictate the future of south Korea.

When the US forces arrived in Korea, they immediately began to transform and organize the nationalist leadership into the Korean Democratic Party (KDP). In October 1945, the US installed Syngman Rhee as the KDP leader, and later as the first President of the Republic of Korea (South Korea). The Seoul leadership was based on a conservative, pro-Western elite with urban roots. This Westernized leadership had a following among the wealthy and the

educated. The division of the Korean Peninsula was
accepted as fact when the Republic of Korea (ROK)
was proclaimed an independent state on 15 August
1948.

The Seoul elite organized itself with massive US
assistance, as well as through mob violence on the
part of various "Youth" groups. Most violent of these
was the Northwest Youth Organization, an organization drawing membership from youth in the Seoul and
central Korea area whose roots were in the northwestern parts of the Korean peninsula (a fact that would
soon have strategic ramifications).

Meanwhile, the fledgling North Korean security
forces were suppressing the Christian population in
North Korea because they were perceived to be Westernized and relatively liberal. They were not expected
to join the Stalinist regime. In 1948-1950, on the pre-
tense of helping these Christians, the Seoul-based
Northwest Youth Organization actively supported a
popular uprising in northwestern and northeastern
Korea, especially the coastal provinces. Because of
their importance to the consolidation of the pro-Western regime in Seoul, the Northwest Youth Organization was able to drag Seoul into actively supporting
the uprising in North Korea.

Almost immediately after World War II, efforts by
the Seoul-based elite to consolidate their hold over
the countryside were running into difficulties. The
reason was the People's Committees' insistence on
retaining their allegiance to the communists, as well
as keeping their arms. Armed clashes spread rapidly
and became a major revolt in the countryside; peak-
ing quickly. It was suppressed by force by the end of
1946.

As relative freedom returned to South Korea, the veteran left sought political recognition in the new Korean government in Seoul. They organized as the South Korean Labor Party (SKLP). However, it was not long before their naive leadership was infiltrated by Soviet-North Korean agents. By mid 1948, the SKLP was under the North's control and was being used as an instrument to penetrate and subvert Seoul from within.

Consequently, early signs of secret organizations in the southern parts of Korea resumed. Having just put down the revolt of 1946, the leadership in Seoul and US advisers would not take any chances. The South Korean security forces overreacted and lumped together all the leftists as agents of the North, thus depriving Seoul the support of the leftist-democratic forces.

Exploiting the growing bitterness of the Korean rural youth, a coalition of militant leftists and North Korean agents organized and equipped a new guerrilla army in the South called the *Inmin-Gun* (People's Army). In 1948, in the first stage of build-up, the People's Army was already 3,000-4,000 strong. An attack was launched in early 1948 (1 March, a symbolic date) on Cheju-Do (Island) and in the Kwangju and Chinju areas in the southern-most tip of the Korean Peninsula. By October 1948, both provinces were in flames, as rebel forces seized control of the city of Yosu and its harbor.

The stories of their initial success encouraged other groups to rise up against Seoul. Consequently, the size of the rebel forces increased markedly, becoming tens of thousands strong. In some places, the expansion was so rapid that the communist agents had problems keeping up with unit establishment and supply of weapons. Indeed, some rebels were sent to fight with bamboo spears. Widespread insurgency and guerrilla warfare grew in early 1948 and continued until 1950, the outbreak of Korean War. By the spring of 1950, the entire center of South Korea was riddled with a rapidly escalating rural revolt and a host of irregular special forces organized from the North. Seoul lost control over vast segments of wild forests and villages.

7

THE ROAD TO THE
KOREAN WAR

For Moscow, Beijing, and Pyongyang, the Korean War was merely a necessary step in a global Communist revolution. The concept of North Korea as the front line of the communist world still haunts Kim Il-Song and the Pyongyang elite. The lessons of the Korean War still guide North Korean policy. It is therefore imperative to understand the war from their point of view.

After World War II, Moscow anticipated a confrontation with the West in the Pacific rim region. The US was occupying Japan and the situation in China was deteriorating rapidly. Consequently, the USSR decided to reactivate The High Command of Troops of the Far East on 22 May 1947. Marshal SU R.Ya. Malinovskiy, who had been the commander of the Transbaykal Front in the 1945 Manchurian Campaign, was nominated as the Commander in Chief.

The primary objective of the new High Command

was to prepare the Soviet Union and its allies for the anticipated major war with the United States. In 1946-47, Moscow was convinced that massive American and Western forces would soon intervene in China in order to save the Nationalist regime. As the PLA was making its first advances, it was inconceivable in Moscow that Washington would let China fall into Communist hands. But Moscow was committed to bolstering the Chinese communist forces and was also determined to secure their control over Manchuria.

The civil war in China continued to escalate, and the Nationalist forces were suffering repeated defeats. The air forces of the Far East High Command, equipped with brand new MiG-9s and MiG-15s, provided air support for an invasion into the Xinkiang on 5 June 1947 and again during the escalation in fighting in northern China in January 1948. A strong reaction by the United States was anticipated in Moscow.

As the Nationalist forces were withdrawing to Taiwan, vowing to return, the USSR and the fledgling PRC announced open military cooperation following the proclamation of the People's Republic of China on 1 October 1949.

A major component of this early cooperation was the defense of southern China, blocking any invasion attempts. In 1949-1950, large Soviet Air Force units provided air cover for Shanghai, East China's industrial center, engaging in aerial combat with US and Nationalist forces. According to the official Soviet history, "Flights by Americans and by forces of Chiang Kai-shek were disrupted. They were given a stern lesson by Soviet air aces." By now, the High Command of Troops of the Far East was rushing reinforcements and supplies into the region.

In 1948, Moscow decided to test the US' determination to defend its strategic assets. Moscow selected Korea as the test site because in 1947 the US had declared that Korea was of "little strategic value to the United States." George F. Kennan wrote that Washington should give up on a democratic South Korea because the US "cannot count on native [South Korean] forces to help hold the line against Soviet expansion. Since the territory is not of decisive strategic importance to us, our main task is to extricate ourselves without too great a loss of prestige."

However, the growing involvement of the US military advisors in fighting the insurgency in South Korea seemed to Moscow to be in contradiction with Washington's declared policy. Therefore, the USSR considered war in Korea to be a major test of Washington's resolve to defend its interests in the Far East. Moscow also needed a strategic diversion to pull the U.S. away from supporting an effort by the Chinese Nationalists to destabilize the fledgling Communist regime in Beijing. In 1949, anticipating a swift victory, Moscow encouraged Kim Il-Song to invade South Korea as such a diversion.

Moscow's preparations for the Korean War began in February 1949. Kim Il-Song met with Stalin, and returned with a host of economic assistance programs, as well as a secret military agreement urging Kim Il-Song to go to war. Committed to the principle of unification by force, he was happy to oblige. As a result of these discussions, by 1950, North Korea was well advanced toward becoming "a Republic of the USSR." But once the USSR secured control over China and North Korea, the annexation process was ultimately abolished.

In the meantime, a flow of Soviet military assistance began. The size of the KPA increased to 200,000 troops. 120,000 were organized into 10 Divisions, 3 regiments each; 62,000 were organized in Special Forces units, and 9,000 in Landing Forces (Marines). The KPA arsenal increased accordingly, reaching 242 T-34 tanks, 176 SU-76 self-propelled guns, as well as 552 heavy artillery barrels (172 122mm & 380 76mm).

Since 1946, Pyongyang has been convinced that unification is possible only through invasion and war, and stated so in no uncertain terms. During his numerous high level consultations with Soviet officials, including meetings with Stalin in Moscow in February 1949, Kim Il-Song repeatedly advocated the use of force and the establishment of a single communist Korea. Therefore, once Stalin instructed Pyongyang to invade the South, it was only natural that Kim Il-Song and his loyalists were genuinely eager to comply.

The communists portrayed the war as a liberation of their brethren in distress. In the spring of 1949, once Kim Il-Song returned from Moscow, the North Koreans began to escalate the guerrilla warfare in the South to the point of direct involvement in the fighting.

The rebellion inside South Korea expanded to include a localized border war along the 38th parallel. In the same period, mainly from September 1949 to March 1950, the DPRK sent over 3,000 guerrillas, 600 of them highly trained, to organize local forces and escalate warfare. In the spring of 1949, the South's forces began maneuvering to block infiltration from the North while DPRK special forces and local guerrillas tried to protect their supply routes.

Consequently, ever larger forces of both South and North Korea were thrown into these engagements. The worsening winter weather of 1949/50 resulted in a sharp decline of border clashes but the spring of 1950 saw a quick revival of border fighting. The peak in the intensity of fighting was in March-April 1950.

In the spring of 1950, the guerrilla fighting in the center of South Korea became extremely brutal and American forces were drawn into active participation in the fighting.

In the early summer of 1950, the US-assisted South Korean forces were succeeding in suppressing the revolts in the heartland. Consequently, there was an escalation in cross-border fighting as the North was trying to send in reinforcements. In some of the ensuing clashes along the 38th Parallel, some 1,000-2,000 troops of each side were involved. However, soon afterwards, there was a sharp decline in fighting for more than a month sufficient to attract attention in Seoul towards domestic instability and away from the gathering clouds of war.

Meanwhile, there was a marked escalation of military build-up and Soviet aid in southern China. The pace of Chinese mobilization increased, military training intensified, and other indications of military readiness were apparent to the point that British intelligence (SIS) was predicting a Chinese invasion of Taiwan in the summer of 1950. The British intelligence assessment relied heavily on material sent over from Seoul where the representative of the SIS was George Blake, a KGB spy.

Blake could not ignore the flow of information about a military build-up in China. But on Moscow's instructions, he must have provided the explanation

that the huge build-up in the PRC was in connection
with a crisis with Taiwan, manufactured to divert attention from a potential crisis in Korea. Furthermore,
Guy Burgess, also a KGB agent, was monitoring the
Far East in the Foreign Office, again interpreting in-
coming information to fit Moscow's needs. Finally,
Kim Philby, yet another KGB agent, was the SIS liaison with the CIA in Washington, implementing the
special relationship between the two services at that
time. All of these KGB agents, and perhaps others as
well, contributed to the distortion of the Western intelligence understanding of the region.

By now, the Chinese were indeed committed to
war. Most important were arrangements made in Manchuria with senior commanders such as Lin Biao, who
made a commitment to the Koreans, even before Mao
was notified and Beijing officially approved the PLA's
participation in the war. Ultimately, in August 1950,
the PRC formally agreed to intervene in the Korean
war provided the USSR supply modern arms and especially fighter aircraft. As the war escalated, Soviet
aid to China more than tripled. The USSR primarily
used Chinese forces early on in the war.

8

WAR IN KOREA

On 25 June 1950, fighting erupted around 3-4 am with a massive artillery barrage from across the North Korean border. Soon afterwards the invasion of major KPA units in four main thrusts began. Moscow, Beijing, and Pyongyang were all convinced that the war would be short, and that the US would not intervene beyond some symbolic show of force. This opinion persisted until late September 1950 after the landing in Inchon which, for the first time, gave the Soviets and the Chinese a clear understanding of the US/ UN resolve. (see fig.3)

Although the KPA had the advantage of surprise on 25 June 1950, the resistance of South Korean forces was intense. However, with so few forces and little or no heavy weapons, they could not block the Northern assault. Seoul fell to the North Koreans on the 29th. The next day, President Truman ordered General MacArthur to commit US forces stationed in Japan to block the North Koreans. The first American units arrived in Korea on July 1st. These US forces were

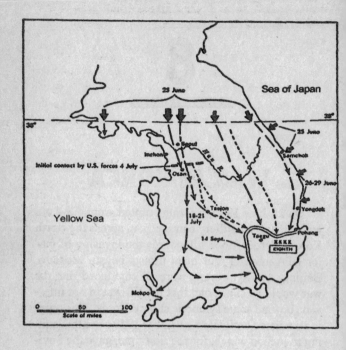

The following labels appear on the map:

25 June

Sea of Japan

38°

25 June

38°

Inchon

Seoul

Initial contact by U.S. forces 4 July

Samchok

Yellow Sea

Osan

26-29 June

Taejon

Yongdok

18-21 July

Taegu

Pohang

14 Sept.

EIGHTH

Mokpo

0   50   100
Scale of miles

Fig 3 — The first phase of the Korean War: The initial thrust of
the KPA, pushing the US and ROK forces all the way back to
the Pusan perimeter in the southern tip of the peninsula.

unable to contain the North Korean assault, and in early August, were pushed into a small area in the southern tip of the peninsula known as the Pusan Perimeter.

The rapid advance of the KPA and their speedy entry into Seoul gave a boost to the various communist and leftist guerrilla forces still in the heartland of South Korea. Encouraged and assisted by the North Korean special forces which had previously infiltrated the South, the guerrillas continued their active participation in the fighting. They played an important role in the occupation of Seoul and the organization of rallies, for the benefit of the world's media, welcoming the KPA units as liberators. Expertly led bands attacked the Southern lines of communication and disrupted transportation, especially during the critical time of the Pusan perimeter. Furthermore, as stories and myths of the rebel activities spread, many uncertain South Korean youth decided to evade mobilization. Consequently, the South Korean forces were deprived of numerous able-bodied soldiers and the US had to deploy American troops instead. Despite the allocation of large allied forces, guerrilla activities did not subside until after the end of the Korean war.

However, in mid September, the North Korean lines collapsed, and a withdrawal northward began. By the end of September, US/UN forces crossed the 38th Parallel into North Korean territory and began a quick advance northwards.

The Inchon landing was a clear demonstration of the US/Western determination to save the South but Moscow knew early on about the West's intentions to overthrow the Pyongyang regime in the North from US reports to the UN, as well as from Philby in Washington. Those intentions were confirmed once US/UN forces crossed the 38th parallel under a UN mandate to reunify Korea. The thought that a communist regime could be destroyed by force of arms was totally unacceptable to Moscow, Beijing and, for obvious reasons, Pyongyang.

Soviet preparations to meet the anticipated escalation had begun even before the Inchon landing. Already in early-September 1950, Gen.Col. Antonov and a large Soviet staff helped the PLA 4th Army HQ in Shenyang prepare for war. Once the fighting broke out and the US resolve had been demonstrated, the USSR mobilized its forces in the Far East and started to rush reinforcements to the area. Although the Soviet Union made an effort not to get involved in the ground fighting in Korea, it nevertheless prepared to send five divisions into Korea to help the DPRK defeat the US had the situation deteriorated. Soviet forces significantly increased their direct involvement once China joined the war.

Stalin was putting pressure on Mao Zedong to commit Chinese forces to the battle. At the same time, separate arrangements with PLA in Manchuria were being made so these forces would be ready for immediate intervention. These preparations were taking place when events in South Korea did not yet indicate the US/UN intention to cross the 38th parallel.

Chinese forces began slipping into North Korea just as the first US forces crossed the 38th parallel. In early October 1950, Lin Biao directed the infiltration of over 300,000 Chinese troops into North Korea. Lin Biao owed a lot to the Koreans from the days of the Chinese Civil War. The Chinese troops would cross the Yalu at night, moving only during darkness to selected concealed staging areas located in caves and heavily wooded areas. The Chinese troops marched some 20 miles each night, hiding during the day. This concealed reinforcement continued after the direct engagements between Chinese and US troops on November 5-8, 1950. The PRC admits that its forces crossed the Korean border on October 25th. However, only on November 12th did the Chinese government announce that it would permit "volunteers" to participate in the fighting in Korea. All together, the Chinese forces included 30 infantry divisions and 4 artillery divisions by late 1950.

Meanwhile, the USSR was escalating its own direct, though secret, involvement in the war. The most critical contribution of the USSR to the war effort of the PRC and the DPRK was the direct involvement of the Soviet Air Force, and the overall command, advisory and logistical support for the PRC-DPRK armed forces. In 1950, Soviet crack aviation divisions deployed to Manchuria, and provided dependable air cover against US air attacks. In that capacity, the Soviet fighters repeatedly engaged US fighters. The USSR also provided the KPA and the PLA with an uninterrupted supply of weapons, ammunition, fuel, food, and medicine.

The deployment of MiG-15s into the Mukden area and the training of Chinese pilots began in September 1950. At first, the Soviet MiG-15s were a part of a generally defensive deployment for the protection of Manchuria. The first 6-9 MiG-15s appeared along the Yalu River and unsuccessfully attacked USAF F-51s on 1 November 1950. A few days later, the MiG-15s attacked B-29s on a deep bombing strike.

Meanwhile, the US/UN ground forces overwhelmed the North Koreans, and swiftly advanced into the North. In late October 1950, the US forces occupied Pyongyang, and toward the end of the month, virtually the entire territory of North Korea. (see fig.4)

By now, the Chinese build-up in Manchuria was too huge to be concealed. Indeed, by mid October, US intelligence noted the presence of 38 PLA divisions in Manchuria with reinforcements arriving daily. By the end of the month, the US intelligence estimate stood at 200,000 troops while, in reality, the size of PLA deployment was closer to 380,000-400,000 troops. However, US intelligence failed to note the on-going infiltration of Chinese forces into Korea, as well as the extent of involvement of Soviet forces in the war.

Thus when the first US-Chinese clashes took place in early November, they came as a complete surprise. By the end of November, US forces were pushed southwards to a defense line in central North Korea. By then massive reinforcements had arrived from China, and the PLA began a series of "human wave" offensives under extremely harsh weather conditions that simply overwhelmed the US/UN forces. Even though Chinese and North Korean infantry suffered tremendous casualties in the process, the communists continued to push the US/UN forces southwards. By late December 1950, US/UN forces were once again south of the 38th parallel and on the retreat. Seoul fell again to the North Korean forces. It was not until late January 1951, that the US/UN forces, relying on large-scale reinforcements, were able to stabilize a defense line in central South Korea.

A counter-offensive started soon afterwards, and within a month, US/UN forces returned to Seoul. By

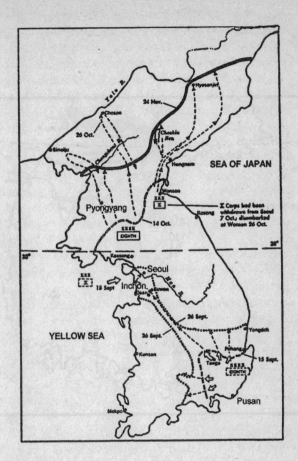

Fig 4 — The second phase of the Korean War: The offensive of the US/UN forces up north, all the way to the Chinese border, and their subsequent withdrawal under PLA pressure.

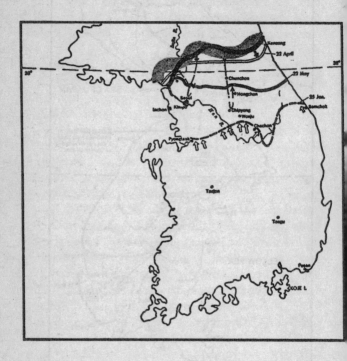

Fig 5 — The third phase of the Korean War: The prolonged and bloody stalemate in central Korea leading to the emergence of the DMZ.

mid April 1951, after a series of massive engagements, the US/UN forces stabilized a line slightly north of the 38th parallel. By the summer of 1951, PLA/KPA forces in Korea numbered 460,000. From then until the cease-fire agreement was signed on 27 July 1953, the front remained essentially static. This line still constitutes the DMZ that separates North and South Korea. (see fig.5)

During the Korean War, the Soviet High Command exercised control from command posts in Mukden and Antung. Although nominally belonging to the PLA, the Allied Joint Headquarters in Antung was actually run by the Soviet "advisors" who were present in, and in charge of, the control room at all times. Chinese officers anticipated an escalation of Soviet direct involvement. They were told that the USSR would send air force and artillery support. However, Soviet presence became predominant in the air. The DPRK's air force was basically Chinese with Russian pilots in all leading positions. Soviet squadrons were being rotated through the front at about six-week intervals to enable as large a number of Soviet MiG-15 pilots as possible to acquire combat experience against the US F-86s. The Soviets claim that during their involvement in the Korean War, "dozens of American aircraft were destroyed in the air by Soviet pilots."

One of the most important contributions of the USSR was the organization of a SIGINT (signals intelligence) system that intercepted USAF radio traffic. The analysis of the radio communication permitted the identification of impending strikes, their character, location and direction. The Soviet Air Force relied on this information to organize large-scale ambush operations.

Strategic bombers were neutralized and Allied losses were heavy but the US claimed a great victory on the basis of a highly favorable aerial kill ratio between the F-86s and the MiG-15s. All together, UN air forces lost a total of 147 aircraft to enemy aircraft and claimed a total of 900 confirmed kills. The USAF F-86s claimed 810 enemy aircraft, 792 of them MiG-15s. The USAF losses in aerial combat reached 139, including 78 F-86s. This makes a F-86:MiG-15 kill ratio of about 10:1. Nikita Khrushchev would later point out that the Soviet leadership was fully aware of their defeat in the air: "Our MiG-15s were simply outclassed and began to suffer defeat. We lost our dominance in the air. The Americans could cut through our air defenses and bomb North Korea with impunity."

The Korean War ended with a cease fire declared on 27 July 1953 with the UN and Communist forces deployed roughly along the 38th Parallel, the same lines they had held back in 1950. When the fighting ended in the summer of 1953, the US had suffered 34,000 KIA, 105,000 wounded, and hundreds of POWs taken to the USSR for interrogation where they vanished. British Commonwealth forces suffered 1,300 KIA and some 5,000 wounded. The ROK forces suffered 59,000 KIA and 291,000 wounded. The PRC/DPRK suffered over 500,000 KIA and over 1,000,000 wounded.

Both Koreas and their allies significantly upgraded their military capabilities during the war years. Now, there were two huge armed groupings tensely confronting each other along the DMZ, eager and ready to complete the sacred mission of unification. In Pyongyang, Kim Il-Song was adamant that the struggle for unification must continue at all cost. Since that time, he has sacrificed the development and well being of his country in the pursuit of the capability to carry out this task.

PART II

THE RISE OF THE NORTH KOREAN MILITARY MIGHT

Shrouded in self-imposed isolation and secrecy, North Korea has succeeded in building the world's fourth largest armed force, the world's third largest chemical warfare force, a large stockpile of chemical and biological weapons, and already some six nuclear weapons in operational status. At present, the DPRK is one of the prime sources of ballistic missiles and nuclear, biological, and chemical (NBC) weapons expertise and technology throughout the Third World.

Pyongyang is convinced that they would win a new war. Generations of young North Koreans have grown up knowing no other objective in life but to sacrifice their lives for the historic mission of the Great Leader, Kim Il-Song. The combination of their zeal with the huge quantities of weapons at their disposal makes North Korea a serious threat today.

9

THE RISE OF THE
NORTH KOREAN
MILITARY MIGHT

North Korea's development of warfare capability is in line with their traditional belief in the need to expand the reach of communism throughout the world by force. This goal has only intensified since the early 1960s, when Pyongyang began to notice a gap between the pace of their own development and that of the South. In 1963, Kim Il-Song insisted on arming his forces with "the most advanced weapons."

When the military build-up began in earnest in the early 1960s, Pyongyang was determined to prepare itself for a total war with its enemies. Therefore, the objective was the overall militarization of society, not just the armed forces. It is Kim Il-Song's objective to make every North Korean an active participant in what he is convinced will be the inevitable war for the liberation of the South. In early 1963, Pyongyang de-

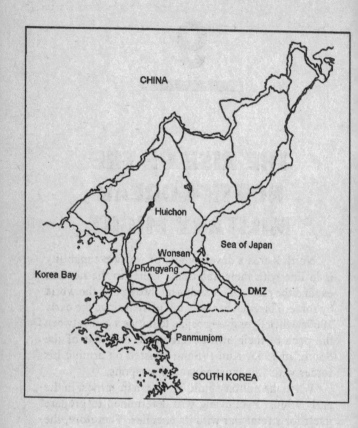

CHINA

Huichon

Sea of Japan

Wonsan

Phongyang

Korea Bay

DMZ

Panmunjom

SOUTH KOREA

Fig 6 — The road network of North Korea

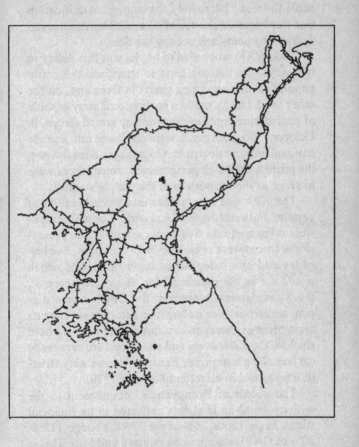

Fig 7 — The railway system of North Korea

cided "to strengthen the People's Army still more, arm all the people, and turn the territory into an impregnable fortress." Ultimately, the strategy of unification war was based on the use of all available resources to defeat the enemy and occupy the South.

The DPRK proceeded to implement this policy in two ways. On the one hand to transform the entire population into an armed guerrilla force and, on the other hand, build a modern professional army capable of confronting contemporary enemy armed forces. In October 1966, both trends were combined into a single national military doctrine. According to Kim Il-Song, the professional high performance armed forces were to serve as the foundation of the people's army.

The KPA was reorganized into a combination of popular units and professional units. The main forces were organized into five "mass armies": The professional forces were organized in 19 divisions, five brigades and one independent regiment, all of which would act as the spearhead for, and quality core of, the Mass Armies. Moreover, the DPRK began digging numerous deep underground storage sites for its main offensive weapon systems so that they are both shielded from discovery and attack, and are ever ready for launching a surprise offensive. This military structure remained in effect until around 1970.

The extent of Pyongyang's commitment to the military build-up is clearly reflected in its financial status. In the 1960s, 30% of the DPRK's budget (15%-20% of GNP) was spent on military build-up. This is a huge allocation when considering that the KPA received most of its weapons essentially for free (either as gifts or as very long-term loans not payable for several years and with little or no interest).

In early 1965, marked improvement of relations with the USSR resulted in a flow of high performance weapons into North Korea, including the MiG-21, then the hottest fighter in the Soviet arsenal. By 1968, the KPA had completed a major modernization through the introduction of large quantities of late model weapon systems from the USSR. Furthermore, North Korean mid-rank and senior officers were sent to higher military schools and academies in the USSR to learn the principles of contemporary warfare. Consequently, by 1970, by conservative estimate, DPRK had some 415,000 men under arms plus 1,250,000 reserves, as well as 25,000 in the security forces and border guards. The KPA was equipped with 900 tanks, 6,000 towed artillery pieces and 200 SPGs. Four submarines were key to a growing fleet. The air force had 580 combat aircraft, all post-1950s jet models, including 70 Il-28 medium bombers and 90 MiG-21s. They also had 300 SA-2s in 60 sites. (As will be discussed below, this acquisition led to a SAM-to-SSM conversion.)

The Soviet Union's guarantees of the survival of the regime in Pyongyang and the knowledge that Moscow would not permit a strategic defeat encouraged North Korea's aggressive planning to incite a popular war in the South. At first, the DPRK was apprehensive about the reaction of the US and ROK, especially in view of US aggressiveness demonstrated in Vietnam and Taiwan.

However, once the Soviet guarantees were given in mid 1965, Pyongyang unleashed a campaign of guerrilla and terrorist war against the South to provoke an uprising of the people. Indeed, between 1965 and 1970, North Korea launched a series of daring special forces strikes and infiltration efforts. These strikes peaked with the January 1968 attack by a 31-man commando unit on the South Korean Presidential Palace (the Blue House) in Seoul, in an attempt to assassinate President Park. Ultimately, the DPRK failed to incite genuine revolt in the South, or even gain an active following. Meanwhile, the USSR and the PRC became apprehensive about possible US reaction as the war in Vietnam was escalating.

As military knowledge about contemporary warfare was being accumulated, the DPRK continued to expand their weapon systems. In 1969, Kim Il-Song urged the further development and acquisition of weapons modified specifically for the peculiarities of the Korean peninsula. The internal development of weapons and mass production capabilities were accomplished at great expense to the DPRK's economy. According to Ko Yong-Hwan, a recent high-level defector, the highest levels in Pyongyang concluded in the mid 1980's that they "could not cope with the situation with conventional (classic) weapons" and consequently Pyongyang knowingly sacrificed the national economy in exchange for large-scale NBC weapons capabilities.

Soviet influence on North Korea's warfare strategy was obvious. The KPA would use conventional warfare methods at first but would be prepared to employ weapons of mass destruction should conventional warfare fail to achieve results. Indeed, the North Korean national strategy and the structure of the military are based on the work of Soviet military experts since the mid 1950s. The USSR considered the Korean peninsula as the most strategically unstable conflict spot in the Far East and the focal point of the

East-West confrontation in that region. In the DPRK was a communist leader committed to the realization of the Marxist-Leninist Revolution through the forced unification of Korea and any eruption of fighting on the peninsula would inevitably escalate into the direct involvement of the Soviet Armed Forces.

Soviet military analysts attributed that dangerous situation to the conditions in South Korea. They considered ROK to be "one of the most important bulwarks of the imperialist policy in the Far East and South East Asia," and therefore the source of permanent military danger. The Soviet High Command defined the primary source of danger as the duality of forces deployed in South Korea. On the one hand, there were the highly capable ROK Armed Forces that were implementing Seoul's policies and directives. On the other hand, there were more than 40 American military bases in South Korea. The experts in Moscow were apprehensive of the "special danger" in this situation, pointing out that DPRK aggression could incite an automatic reaction by the US, and, in quick succession, the USSR and the PRC, thus starting a new World War. The Soviets were genuinely worried that any local incident in Korea might escalate into a global confrontation .

Moscow was encouraged by a series of acts of "self-restraint" demonstrated by the US in the wake of North Korean provocations. These acts of aggression included the February 1968 capture of the USS *Pueblo* (a US Navy vessel used for the collection of SIGINT) in international waters, the April 1969 shooting down of an EC-121 (a USAF transport plane converted for the collection of SIGINT) by North Korean MiG-17s, and a series of clashes across the DMZ initiated by the KPA in which 21 Americans were killed.

These provocations had a dual-purpose. The first and more obvious objective was to test the limit of US patience and self-restraint. The clashes along the DMZ were the primary instrument. The other and more significant objective was to significantly reduce the US' ability to collect electronic intelligence. Such interference with US intelligence collection was considered critical for the concealment of the extent of the massive military build-up planned for the 1970s.

Senior KGB experts had been preparing for the seizure of the USS *Pueblo* for several months. They planned and executed the electronic trap that lured it into the ambush of the North Korean Navy. The Soviet experts personally removed and studied the *Pueblo*'s sophisticated electronic gear, and interrogated the American crew. The *Pueblo* proved extremely valuable for the USSR. Commander Lloyd Bucher, the *Pueblo*'s captain, later conceded that there was little about his ship that the North Korean captors and Soviet interrogators had not already known, thus reflecting the thoroughness of the Soviet-Korean preparations for the operation. The EC-121 was shot down by the MiG-17s as a follow-up to the *Pueblo* seizure, in order to deter the US from using an airborne substitute for SIGINT collection.

10

BUILDING A MODERN ARMY

In the early 1970s, military experts in both Pyongyang and Moscow closely studied the aftermath and lessons of the 1968-69 clashes in Korea. For the Soviet military analysts, the meaning of the "self-restraint" clearly demonstrated by Washington was that the leadership of the United States would most likely deliberate for some time before deciding on a reaction to a major provocation in the Korean peninsula. After all, it took Washington five days to decide on its reaction to the North Korean invasion of 1950. Moscow was determined to ensure that if a major confrontation did take place in Korea, their objectives would be attained prior to Washington's ability to decide on a proper and meaningful reaction. In other words, North Korean victory would need to be achieved in what the Soviets define as "the initial period of war." The combination of these considerations determined the Soviet posture on the Korean peninsula, and, in turn, the structure and doctrine of the North Korean Armed Forces.

The KPA absorbed growing quantities of modern weapons from both the USSR and the PRC and trained their units in the latest tactics. Bunkers and tunnels were built to protect the DPRK's weapons from all possible threat including US nuclear strikes. In addition, a series of tunnels, estimated to number as many as 25 or so, were dug under the DMZ to facilitate the infiltration of commandos, special forces, and terrorists into South Korea. (see fig.8) By 1979, the KPA had 675,000 standing troops and 2,500,000 trained reservists and their arsenal included 2,300 tanks, 3,500 pieces of artillery, 1,300 MBRLs (Multiple-Barrel Rocket Launchers), 565 combat aircraft, 90 amphibious craft, and 15 submarines. This was a tremendous jump in size and quality from 1970.

Although the North Koreans continued to conceal their build-up in order enhance the surprise factor, they felt a large surprise attack was no longer crucial for success. The DPRK's declared doctrine for war was very specific in its predictions about the course of a war with the South, leading to the ultimate unification of Korea. Kim Il-Song explained in late April 1975: "If Revolution takes place in South Korea, we, as one and the same nation, will not just look at it with folded arms but will strongly support the South Korean people. If the enemy ignites war recklessly, we shall resolutely answer it with war and completely destroy the aggressors. In this war we will only lose the military demarcation line and will gain the country's reunification." Left unsaid was Pyongyang's intention to incite the "popular war" that, in turn, would lead to the start of the major war.

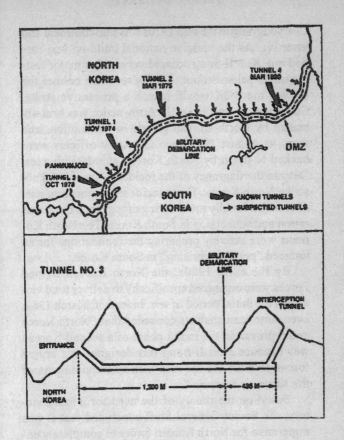

Fig 8 — The extensive tunnel system the DPRK built in order to clandestinely insert special forces into the ROK. The location of the still undiscovered tunnels is based on defectors' reports and other sources. Note that the location of the discovered tunnels fit closely with the overall distribution of tunnels. The cutaway of one of the discovered tunnels demonstrates how they were dug under mountain ridges to shield their existence, including the noise of digging, from the US/ROK forces.

Pyongyang in the mid 1970s was self-confident and assertive. As the massive national build-up was carried out, Kim Il-Song ordered yet another major testing of US self-restraint to make sure that neither the US nor the ROK would launch a preventive strike. Consequently, in 1975 a US Army major was brutally beaten by North Korean guards in Panmunjon, and then, in August 1976, two US Army officers were hacked to death by North Korean guards with axes. Despite the flagrancy of the incidents, the US did not strike North Korea. These incidents occurred in parallel with a rapidly intensifying propaganda blitz, agitation and subversion in South Korea. The North Koreans were actively preparing the foundations for an induced "popular uprising" in South Korea.

By the early 1980s, the North Korean Armed Forces were organized specifically to deliver total victory in the initial period of war. Indeed, in March 1982, even American analysts conceded that "North Korea could prevail in the initial phase of a second Korean war because Kim Il-Song has designed his armed forces to meet the specific tactical requirements of the Korean peninsula."

Based on the theory of the need for a rapid victory, the Soviet General Staff concluded that it was imperative for North Korean forces to completely encircle the entire peninsula during the initial period of war in order to prevent US intervention in the war. Toward this end, the KPA was organized and equipped for offensive military operations that were ideally suited to conditions on the peninsula. The Soviet High Command was convinced that their best chance for victory was to occupy the peninsula before U.S. forces could intervene. This belief was based on Soviet strategic analysis of the Korean War (see fig. 9 & 10)and was reinforced by the results of the "tests" of American resolve in the late 1960s and mid-1970s. The Soviet analysis stressed the importance of the very existence of the Pusan perimeter to Washington's decision to pursue and escalate the war in Korea in the summer of 1950. The senior analysts on the Soviet General Staff concluded that it was imperative for North Korean forces to surround the entire peninsula during the initial period of war in order to prevent (or greatly reduce) the US ability to intervene, escalate and expand the hostilities.

The North Koreans completed the first phase of their military build-up only by the early 1980s, when they finally felt they could meet virtually any military contingency on the peninsula. The KPA now had all the tools required for a deep, lightening offensive. By 1985, Moscow fully expected the KPA to handle all strategic challenges. Soviet analysis said, "the Korean People's Army has a greater responsibility than ever before to maintain peace and security in the region." Moscow described the KPA as being "ready at a moment's notice to repulse an attack on their country." Indeed, the deployment and organization of the KPA already committed them to launch a surprise attack straight from the peace time deployment.

One of the key elements of the Soviet Art of War is the conduct of combat operations throughout the entire depth of the enemy forces. The collapse of the enemy is achieved through the combined effect of rapid advance at the front and chaos at the rear. But the terrain of the Korean peninsula would not allow an exceptionally speedy advance. So, the use of diversionary troops in the deep rear of the enemy

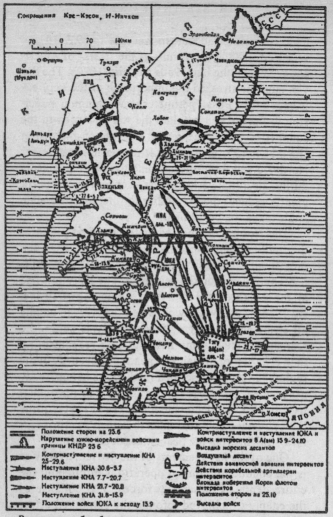

Fig 9 — Soviet Intelligence analysis of the Korean War, phase 1. Note the attention paid to the encirclement effort of the DPRK and the contribution of US/UN naval blockade to the US/UN offensive.

Fig 10 — Soviet Intelligence analysis of the Korean War, phase 2.
Note the emphasis on the PRC's offensives and the infrastructure of airbases in the South.

might decide the war. The DPRK envisions a four-phase war scenario: The first phase is the subversion of South Korea, essentially inducing the popular revolt. The second phase is delivering the strategic shock, primarily through the swift capture of Seoul and the infliction of massive casualties on the enemy. The third phase is the rapid encirclement of the peninsula so that any reinforcements from abroad, namely the US, would have to fight their way into Korea. (Pyongyang is convinced that this would deter the US from further intervening.) The fourth phase is a consolidation of the communist regime through a massive and thorough purge of all undesirable elements of society.

By the early-1980s the KPA had completed the fine tuning of the first phase of its total modernisation of the North Korean military machine. The KPA became the world's sixth largest army. This phase included a massive build-up based on the foundations laid in the late 1970s. By 1982, some 24% of the North Korean GNP was devoted to this military buildup. If dual-use industrial output and construction projects were taken into account, the defense sector consumed more than 30% of the GNP.

The North Koreans deployed major forces in some 100 underground bunkers 12 to 18 miles from the DMZ. Each bunker can accommodate large quantities of troops and supplies. The use of these troops for the breaching of the South Korean forward defenses reduces the advance warning time of the West to 6 hours. The Artillery and the Mechanized Commands are capable of conducting a swift deep offensive in order to encircle the US and ROK forces, and deny the US easy access to Korean territory from the outset of hostilities. The DPRK would then complete the occupation of the South.

By 1984-85, the KPA had standing forces of 785,000 men and some 4,000,000 reservists. Their new reserve system was far more efficient. The reserves were now organized into Task Force Units, each 260,000 strong and organized into 23 infantry divisions with specific missions and training programs to ensure constant operational capabilities. The KPA arsenal included 2,800-3,000 tanks, 4,100-4,200 artillery pieces, 2,000 MBRLs, 740-750 combat aircraft (including the recently acquired MiG-23s and Su-7s), 104 landing craft, 21 submarines, and over 100 FROG-5 and FROG-7 SSMs.

Moreover, the first phase of construction of secret underground forward deployment hardened shelters was completed and the DPRK amassed underground supplies for at least 30 days of very intense total war.

The KPA reorganized into a purely offensive configuration including the mastering of combined-arms units. Some 40 motorized infantry divisions and brigades constituted the bulk of the standing professional armed forces. To spearhead of the offensive, the North Koreans had the rapidly growing Air Force; the Artillery Command with SSMs, heavy tube artillery, mortars, and MBRLs; the Mechanized Command with a deep offensive corps made up of three motorized-rifle divisions, two tank divisions, five tank brigades and two independent tank regiments; and a Navy for coastal warfare.

The basic deployment of the KPA was: the 1st Army Group facing the eastern sector of the DMZ, the 2nd Army Group facing the western sector, and the 5th Army Group covering the central sector. The IV Corps (recently converted from the 4th Army Group) was stationed in the Pyongyang area. Three corps—the III Corps, VI Corps and VIII Corps—were deployed around Wonsan and the coastal regions. Each of these Corps or Army Groups had four infantry divisions and one independent brigade. The exceptions were the 2nd Army Group on the road to Seoul that had five infantry divisions and one independent brigade; and the VII Corps that had three divisions and three brigades. (The difference between Army Group and Corps was that the latter had responsibility for their area of deployment while the former was a combat unit only. Over the next few years, the Army Groups north of the DMZ would be converted into Corps.) In 1985, the III, VI, and VII Corps were ordered to begin organizing high-quality maneuver forces, dominated by fighting vehicles, self-propelled artillery and tanks, that would serve as the core for the theater offensive forces. These units would ultimately become the KPA's Armored and Mechanized Corps.

The most important element of the North Korean Armed Forces were the special forces responsible for deep infiltration into the South in order to incite the "popular revolt" that would provide justification for the KPA's offensive. They were organized as the 124th Army under the Special 8th Corps. In the early 1980s, the 124th Army included 22 diversionary regiments (three battalions each), three commando regiments, five airborne battalions, a river-crossing regiment, and three amphibious battalions. All together, there were over 100,000 special troops in 560 maneuver battalions, constituting some 15% of the North Korean standing Armed Forces. For comparison, back in 1970 the KPA had only 12,000 special forces. The size of the increase is indicative of their growing importance.

The Special 8th Corps also included over 200 An-2 light transport aircraft and 87 US-made Hughes 300 and Hughes 500 helicopters for simultaneous infiltration to the South. The helicopters were illegally purchased in the US and delivered to North Korea via the Netherlands and Japan in a complex clandestine operation of North Korean Intelligence with assistance from the KGB. The South Korean Air Force uses both types of helicopters, and therefore, their ability to block infiltration by Hughes helicopters from the North will be extremely difficult. Indeed, in the summer of 1985, a test penetration into South Korean airspace by two North Korean Hughes 500 helicopters was successful. The North Koreans also developed a fleet of various semi-submersible landing craft for seaborne infiltration. Furthermore, there are on-going persistent efforts to insert agents and diversionary teams by boats, through tunnels under the DMZ, or by air.

It is impossible to estimate the actual number of deep-cover agents already in place. The quality and tenacity of the North Korean diversionary troops was clearly demonstrated in the October 9, 1983, bombing in Rangoon in which North Korean officers attempted to kill the entire leadership of South Korea.

A major reason for the generosity of the Soviet and Chinese military assistance to the KPA was their growing need for a provocative strategic asset in East Asia. Rhetoric aside, Moscow knew perfectly well that South Korea did not threaten the North. The "real threat" from South Korea was its role as a cornerstone for what Moscow defined as "a tripartite military alliance among Washington, Tokyo and Seoul," whose strategic influence stretches into "all areas in the Indian and Pacific Ocean region." Moscow explained that as a result of the cementing of American military ties with Japan and South Korea, Washington could strive "to make the Far East one of the most important lines of the global imperial strategy of Washington." In that context, Moscow was concerned about the growing awareness in Japan about the buildup in the Far East and Tokyo's desire to improve the Japanese defense system. A 1985 Soviet intelligence study of the Armed Forces of Japan emphasized the threat of South Korea and Japan to the peace in the Indian Ocean. The Soviet High Command was especially concerned about the revival of a two-front threat. In 1983, Yuri Andropov warned that "attempts are being made to revive Japanese militarism and to hitch it to the military-political machine of NATO." The emergence of a credible cooperation between NATO and friendly forces in the Far East could seriously interfere with Soviet regional designs.

This regional awareness determined the next phase in the military build-up of the Democratic People's Republic of Korea.

11

NORTH KOREA'S WEAPONS OF MASS DESTRUCTION

North Korea began the development of chemical weapons in the late-1950s with Soviet assistance and expertise. Limitations of the local chemical industry prevented the DPRK from reaching complete production capacity. In a method that currently characterizes most Third World chemical weapons production, North Korea procured the basic components of the chemical weapons from external sources. In the 1960s and 1970s, the DPRK purchased large quantities of "agro-chemicals" from Japan. Meanwhile, internal production capacity improved, bringing the DPRK to near self-sufficiency in the production of basic chemical weapons. Pyongyang increased the production rates of chemical weapons in 1985. In the late-1980s, chemical production was being continually increased in several known locations: Aoji-ri, Chongjin,

Chongsu-Nodongjagu, Hamhung, Hungnam, Kusong, Nampo, Pakchon, Pyongyang, Sinuiju, Sunchon, and Yongan. In addition, the DPRK has three research and development sites and six major storage sites of chemical agents. The DPRK's chemical arsenal includes Sarin, Tabun, Phosgene, Adamsite, the mustard gas family and 'blood agents' such as hydrogen cyanide. Since the early-1990s, annual production of chemical weapons agents is estimated at over 14 tons, and growing. (see fig.11)

Biological warfare research began in the mid-1960s and, since the late-1960s, the DPRK was developing bacteriological weapons. The main weapon development projects are conducted in the Microbic Institute of the Academy of Sciences for Medicine. The North Koreans tested their bacteriological agents on human victims, mainly political prisoners. In the late-1980s, the DPRK had some 10 different strains of bacteria including anthrax, cholera, bubonic plague, smallpox, yellow fever, diphtheria, typhoid fever, tuberculosis, pest-spawned diseases and blood contamination agents. In November 1980, Kim Il-Song ordered the expansion of the program and the development of advanced biological weapons. One of the major roles of the DPRK special forces is to spread large quantities of bacteriological weapons in densely populated areas of South Korea.

The DPRK also acquired sophisticated chemical and biological weapons from the Soviet Union. In mid-1986, the USSR supplied the DPRK with chemical aerial bombs, most likely filled with Sarin. Soon afterwards, the USSR also supplied aerial bombs with "double channel" agents that cause paralysis within 10 seconds and death within 10 minutes.

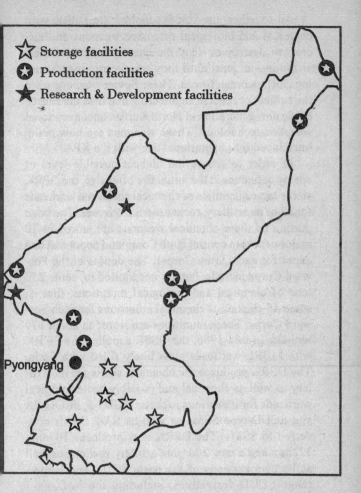

Fig 11 — Chemical and Biological warfare sites in North Korea. Note how dispersed they are, and the numerous storage sites in the immediate proximity of the DMZ which are optimized to serve an offensive against the ROK.

All together, the USSR supplied the DPRK with chemical and biological offensive weapons and aircraft to destroy or deny the enemy the use of their airfields— at least until they are overrun by advancing North Korean forces. These Soviet weapons were the subject of reverse engineering and thus the source of the new generation of North Korean unconventional weapons technology. These weapons are now being introduced into operational use with the KPA.

In order to ensure the highest possible level of enemy casualties in the initial fire offensive, the DPRK stores large quantities of chemical shells and warheads for all of its artillery, rocket and SSM forces. The large portion of these chemical weapons are stored in 10 major depots (a central High Command depot and one depot for each Army Corps). The depots of the Forward Corps include, but are not limited to, some 250 tons of chemical and biological munitions, that is, some 45-62 tons of chemical munitions for each Forward Corps. These munitions are stored in about 170 tunnels. In mid-1986, the USSR supplied the DPRK with MBRL warheads most likely filled with Sarin. The DPRK produces the chemical shells for its artillery as well as chemical and possibly bacteriological warheads for its various rockets: FROG-5, FROG-7A and SCUD-type SSMs as well as SA-2 SAMs converted to SSMs. The DPRK now produces 107mm, 122mm and a new 200+mm artillery rockets, as well as its own versions of the basic SCUD and longer-range SCUD-derivatives, including the *NoDong-1* MRBM.

The size of North Korea's arsenal of weapons of mass destruction, and Pyongyang's determination to use them, were confirmed in late March 1994 by Yi

Chung-Kuk, a former Sergeant in a KPA chemical-warfare unit developing and producing chemical and biological weapons. Yi disclosed that his unit developed a new type of *bio-chemical* weapons which he described as "the most poisonous in the world." They were tested "on living bodies of political prisoners" in several KPA institutions. KPA troops have no doubt that these new weapons—as well as the regular chemical and biological weapons—will be used in a future war on the Korean Peninsula. "Senior officers of our unit told us that we have the strongest toxic weapons in the world and we must be proud of that fact," Yi recalled. He reported that a senior officer told the unit's troops that the DPRK "can kill all the 40 million South Koreans with chemical and biological weapons alone."

12

NORTH KOREA'S BALLISTIC MISSLES

Weapons of mass destruction are useful and effective only if the missiles that carry them can strike their intended targets. At present, ballistic missiles are considered the most effective delivery system in the Third World because although they are not too accurate, they are simple to launch and nearly impossible to stop. Furthermore, the production technologies of basic types of ballistic missiles are within the capabilities of such states as the DPRK. Indeed, North Korea is currently one of the leaders in missile development among the developing countries.

The North Korean missile program owes much of its current capabilities to technological cooperation with the USSR and the PRC. The PRC-DPRK military-technological cooperation began in a series of agreements between 1969 and 1974 concerning the reverse engineering of Soviet naval missiles (mainly SS-N-2 STYX and SS-C-2B SAMLET). Using sample

SS-N-2 missiles provided by North Korea, the Chinese developed their HY-1 model, and, later in the early-1970s, the HY-2 SILKWORM. North Korea assembled HY-1 missiles from parts provided by the PRC. However, by 1974 the DPRK had developed total internal production capacity for the HY-1 and the HY-2. The PRC continues to provide North Korea with up-graded guidance systems for the missiles.

Since the-1970s, the Sino-North Korean cooperation in the conversion and exploitation of Soviet missile technologies was expanded to include the V-75 (SA-2) and various ballistic missiles, mainly the R-65 (FROG 7) and the R-17E (SCUD-B). At first, in 1975, the PRC and the DPRK sought to develop an indigenous tactical missile called the DF-61 but the project proved too challenging. Instead, the DPRK decided on simpler reverse engineering of the Soviet R-17E (SCUD-B) after a few SCUDs had been delivered by Egypt in 1981. The DPRK and the PRC began cooperating in the development of follow-up models to the basic SCUD SSM for the Iranians. In the 1980s, the DPRK had developed its own version of the R-17E, called the NK-SCUD-B, using rocket engines and guidance systems provided by the PRC, and was on the verge of testing a new longer-range ballistic SSM derived from the basic SCUD. Since 1987, the DPRK has been producing 50 NK-SCUD-Bs a year on its main production line in the outskirts of Pyongyang alone.

The first DPRK missile brigade was established in 1985 and deployed in To-Kol, between No-Dong and Chongjin. Equipped with NK-SCUD-Bs, the brigade became fully operational in 1986. In 1988, the DPRK established its second missile unit also equipped with the NK-SCUD-B. The regiment is deployed in the IVth DMZ Corps in south-western North Korea overlooking Seoul.

From 1988-89, the DPRK developed a new longer-range ballistic missile based on SCUD technology, and using key components from the PRC. In the late-1980s, the USSR provided the DPRK with upgraded missile technology and, in June 1991, even transferred at least 10 SCUD-Cs to North Korea for reverse engineering crucial to the production of advanced ballistic missiles. Since then, the DPRK has developed and introduced into operational service a series of these advanced missiles.

First came the NK-SCUD-C which is essentially a stretched-up NK-SCUD-B. Pre-production began in 1989, and the first test launch took place in June 1990 from No-Dong in the direction of Japan. The DPRK was able to complete the development of this mobile SCUD derivative, its primary nuclear SSM, in the fall of 1991. By then, the missile regiment in the IVth DMZ Corps was expanded into a full brigade as a NK-SCUD-C regiment was established in Sari-Won, some 50km north of the DMZ. Meanwhile, a second NK-SCUD-C was test launched by an operational KPA unit in the Kangwon province from its operational position. The SSM flew north-east into the Sea of Japan. Since 1991-92, the rate of production of the NK-SCUD-C has continued to increase for both the KPA and for export to Iran and Syria.

In 1989, the DPRK also began the development of a SCUD-derivative with a range of over 1,000kms. A prototype of this SSM, called the *NoDong-1*, exploded on the launch pad in Tokol around May-June 1990. A successful test launch was completed in early-October 1991 and the SSM became operational and available for export by mid-1992. The DPRK already completed missile launch pads for the *NoDong-1* in Hate (North Hamyong) and Munchon (Kangwon), while a third major missile base is near completion in Chungan near the Chinese border. A mobile version is already in operational status as proven in the test launches in late May 1993. It is installed on both a derivative of the MAZ-543 dedicated TEL vehicle and on special launchers made of Italian-made IVECO heavy trucks, using the Austrian-made TEL system (Palfinger AG is the prime supplier) which is less accurate but much easier to conceal. In late 1993, the KPA already had some 120 *NoDong-1*s and 30 mobile launchers in operational service. (However, the hasty shipments to Iran of some tens of SSMs might have used some of these missiles.)

In late March 1993, the DPRK completed the development of the up-graded *NoDong-1*, "which may be equipped with a nuclear warhead," with 1,300kms range. The DPRK is also accelerating the development of a new *NoDong-2*, estimated to have a range of 1,500-2,000kms. The test launching of the first *NoDong-2* prototypes is expected in 1994-95 and, barring a major set back, the MRBM will become operational in 1996-97.

By early 1994 there was strong evidence that the new generation of North Korean ballistic missiles are far more advanced than recent reports of the *TaepoDong* SSMs suggest. The current DPRK ballistic missile program has four distinct phases (apart from the brief joint Sino-Korean development effort of the DF-61 in 1975-76). (see fig.12)

1. Reverse engineering and modest development

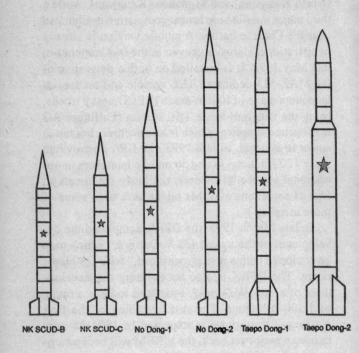

NK SCUD-B   NK SCUD-C   No Dong-1   No Dong-2   Taepo Dong-1   Taepo Dong-2

Fig 12 — The ballistic missiles of North Korea. Note the gradual
development and growth out of the basic SCUD design, and
the subsequent introduction of Chinese technology, resulting
in diverse configurations.

of the basic Soviet R-17E (SCUD-B) into the NK-SCUD-B and NK-SCUD-C.

2. Major upgrading and improvement of the basic Soviet design principles and technologies into medium-range SSMs known as the *NoDong-1*, *NoDong-1* upgrade, and *NoDong-2*.

3. A new generation of two-stage intermediate range ballistic missiles largely based on the integration of relatively advanced, though fully proven, Chinese technoloy — the *TaepoDong-1* and *TaepoDong-2*.

4. A new generation of multiple-stage long range ballistic missiles based on the latest Soviet-Russian and Chinese technologies, known as the *NoDong-X*.

The *NoDong* family of SSMs is very straight forward from an engineering point-of-view. The *NoDong-1* is a direct stretching of the basic NK-SCUD-C in order to reach a range of 1,000 km with a 800 to 1,000 kg warhead. The *NoDong-2* is a result of a several-phased development of the *NoDong-1*. At first, the *NoDong-1* was modified, mainly for Iran, to reach a 1,300 km range and be equipped with a nuclear warhead. The ultimate *NoDong-2* is the result of later refinements of the basic design to strengthen the body of the missile and increase its payload. The *NoDong-2* has a range of over 1,500 km with a 800-1,000 kg warhead, reaching up to 2,000 km with a smaller warhead of 500-800 kg.

The *TaepoDong* family of SSMs are the first of a new generation of two-stage SSMs that rely heavily on integration of relatively advanced and well-tested Chinese missile technology. The most important inputs are mainly pumps for the clustered rocket engines and stage separation technology. Still, the *TaepoDong* SSMs include mainly proven components

of previous SSMs— both Chinese *and* North Korean.
The *TaepoDong-1* has a range of over 2,000 km with
a 1,000 kg warhead. Initial reports suggested that this
missile is a combined *NoDong-1* [first stage] and NK-
SCUD-B/NK-SCUD-C [second stage]. The
TaepoDong-2 has a range of over 3,500 km, also with
a 1,000 kg warhead. According to the same reports,
the *TaepoDong-2* is a 32m long SSM, and has a derivative of the PRC's DF-3/CSS-2 MRBM for its first
stage, and a derivative of the *NoDong-1*—but with a
rounded nosecone—for the second stage. Considering the overall volume of the DF-3-based first stage
of the *TaepoDong-2*, with a small warhead of around
500 kg it can even reach a range of 9,600 km—making it an ICBM. (see fig.13)

However, the *TaepoDong* family of SSMs are actually far more sophisticated and lethal than these reports suggest. The key to the understanding of the
TaepoDong lies in the Iranian ballistic missile development program run jointly with the DPRK and the
PRC since 1990. The main development and production facility of this program is in Isfahan, Iran. Judg-
ing from the overall dimensions and estimated performance, the *TaepoDong-1* is a North Korean version of the the Iranian *Tondar-68* SSM. The *Tondar-
68* is based on Chinese and North Korean technology,
and also the sample missiles provided for test and reverse engineering. Tehran's ultimate objective are two
versions of the *Tondar-68*, the first with a range of
1,200-1,500 km, thus capable of reaching Israel from
launchers inside Iran, and a second with a range of
some 2,000 km to establish regional hegemony.

The *Tondar-68* is a two-stage missile, based on a
Chinese M-11 installed on top of the *Iran-700* , itself

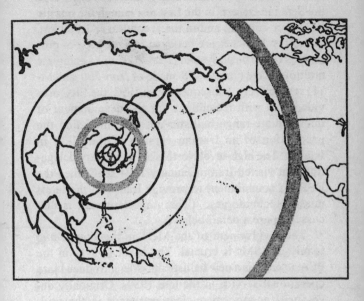

Fig 13 — The reach of the North Korean ballistic missiles, clearly showing their regional and even global impact. The North Korean SSMs, in ascending order of their range, are: NK-SCUD-B; NK-SCUD-C; <u>NoDong-1</u> and upgrades; <u>NoDong-2</u> and <u>TaepoDong-1</u>; <u>TaepoDong-2</u>; <u>NoDong-X</u>.

a derivative of the North Korean *NoDong-1*. In March 1991, Iran test fired the basic *Tondar-68* SSM over the Semnan Desert. In the first test launch the missile flew over 700 km, and in the second over 1,000 km. These test launches are believed to have been of prototypes of the basic system (*Iran-700*) and a complete multiple-stage (*Tondar-68* made of *Iran-700* and M-11) respectively. Subsequently, in 1992, the PRC provided Iran with technology for the development of intermediate-range ballistic missiles, including the production of an Iranian version of the M-11 in Isfahan. The high-level North Korean military delegation that visited Iran in January 1994 reaffirmed the DPRK's commitment to provide Iran with the latest missile technologies. (This important visit is discussed in great detail below.)

The involvement of the M-11 in the *TaepoDong* family of SSMs is crucial. The M-11 (DF-11 in the PLA arsenal) is a new ballistic missile, introduced into operational service in the late 1980s. Originally developed for tactical nuclear warheads in the mid-1980s, the M-11 received HE and CW warheads soon afterwards to meet export demands. The first model of the M-11, with a 135 km range was introduced in 1988. The M-11 soon evolved into a "SCUD substitute" with a comparable range of 290-320 kms with 500-800 kg warhead. The M-11 is a single-stage SSM with solid propellant, and is about the same size as the basic SCUD but with a rounded-up top cone (not a cylinder and cone like the SCUD) to improve aerodynamics and ballistic qualities. The original M-11 has terminal guidance, including an inertial midcourse guidance system, to vastly improve its accuracy. The integration of modern GPS technology, known to have been purchased by the DPRK and the PRC and already installed in the *NoDong-1*, should not be rulled out. Solid fuelled, the M-11 relies on fully mobile TEL vehicles based on the Soviet MAZ-543 TEL vehicle, and can be reloaded and readied for fire in about 45 minutes by a crew fewer than 10. The PRC uses the M-11 as the upper stage in the development of a theater ballistic missile called the M-18. Fully mobile, the M-18 is a "stretched M-11" with two stages of solid fuel.

The installation of the M-11 (or its derivative) as the upper stage of the *TaepoDong* family of SSMs drastically changes the capabilities of these SSMs without really altering their external appearance or dimensions. It is noteworthy that the *TaepoDong-2*'s upper stage was first described as a *NoDong-1* but with a rounded nosecone, a characteristic of the M-11. Solid fuel missiles are far simpler to handle as the upper stage because they are easier to store, do not require fueling, and are less sensitive to separation by explosive-bolts. Most important, of course, is the basic fact that the M-11 is far more accurate and reliable than the *NoDong*. The use of the M-11 as the upper stage means the accuracy and range of the entire *TaepoDong* SSM is dramatically improved. The *TaepoDong-1* is made of an M-11 installed on top of a booster-derivative of the *NoDong-1*, which is basically the principle behind the Iranian *Tondar-68*. In this configuration, the range of over 2,000 km with a 1,000 kg warhead remains unchanged, but the accuracy improves markedly. Similarly, the *TaepoDong-2* is a M-11 installed on top a booster-derivative of the DF-3/CSS-2. Again, the basic range of over 3,500 km with a 1,000 kg warhead remain unchanged. As discussed above, on the basis of the overall size of the *TaepoDong-2*'s DF-3-based booster, it can even reach a range of 9,600 km. The reliabilty and accuracy of the M-11's technological level are crucial for the success of such an ICBM.

Thus, the crucial question concerning the performance, mainly reliability and accuracy, of the *TaepoDong* family of SSMs is the technological basis of the upper stage. There is no doubt that a derivative of the Chinese M-11 markedly improves these performances. The external dimensions of the NK-SCUD, *NoDong* and M-11 SSMs are virtually identical. The key assessing the likelihood of the use of the M-11 in the *TaepoDong* are the facts:

1. The PRC already modified the M-11 as an upper stage for the M-18;

2. The PRC shared this technology with Iran, a lesser ally compared with the DPRK;

3. The DPRK itself is the source of the Soviet-Russian KY-3 solid fuel and guidance technologies that facilitate the marked improvement of the M-11; and

4. North Korean experts, engineers and technicians have been working for several years now with their Chinese counterparts in Isfahan on the *Tondar-68* so that they have already been exposed to the basic M-11 technology.

Therefore, any assessment of the *TaepoDong* family of SSMs must be based on the premise that the upper stage is a derivative of the M-11, which makes for far greater accuracy and reliability.

In assessing the likelihood of the availability of such advanced Chinese strategic technologies in North Korea, it should be stressed that both countries have been cooperating in missile production and development since the early 1970s. Moreover, the DPRK and the PRC now closely cooperate in developing new missiles after signing a series of agreements in 1988, and again in October 1991, which paved the way for joint development of a new generation of missiles. In 1988, the first delegation of 90 North Korean ballistic missile experts was dispatched to the PRC to work on these joint missile projects. Most important among these projects is the development of a MRV-equipped MRBM optimized for nuclear warheads with a range of 800 km. A prototype of this MRBM was successfully test launched in Yinchuan, China, in the fall of 1991.

In 1989-90, the DPRK dispatched some 230 additional military experts from the ground forces, navy and air force to the Dalian base, on the Liaodong peninsula, for cooperation and study of diversified advanced missile technologies—mainly ship-to-ship missiles, various surface-to-surface missiles (both ballistic and cruise), and surface-to-air missiles. In October 1991, during Kim Il-Song's visit to China, the DPRK and the PRC reiterated their commitment to jointly developing ballistic missile technology uniquely applicable for nuclear warheads, especially MRVs and MIRVs.

A major component of the 1991 agreement was Pyongyang's agreement to shop for advance missile technologies to up-grade ballistic missiles in the USSR/CIS and share them with the PRC. Back in the late-1980s, the USSR-DPRK cooperation arrangements were expanded to include advanced SSMs. Indeed, the USSR transferred at least 10 KY-3s (SCUD-Cs) to North Korea in June 1991 for use as samples for reverse engineering crucial to the production of advanced models of ballistic missiles needed to compete with other SSMs on the world market. This shipment also replenished North Korean stockpiles drawn down by exports to the Middle East. Unlike the basic R-17 (SCUD-B), the KY-3 has longer range, solid fuel, and, most importantly, a completely new guidance system with "pinpoint accuracy" that can be adapted to all types of SCUDs and their derivatives. Therefore, the availability of these technologies significantly enhanced the scientific-technological basis of the ballistic missile industry of both North Korea and China. The KY-3 technologies would be ideal for, and easy to integrate with, the M-11-type ballistic missiles to vastly improve their performance.

At present, the PRC is developing a mobile intercontinental ballistic missile capable of striking at the continental US. The Sino-Korean MRBM is used as the basis for the ICBM's upper stage. This ICBM relies heavily on Soviet technology, mainly that of the rail-based SS-24 and the vehicle-based SS-25 ICBMs. Although the original range of the Soviet ICBMs is around 10,000 kms, the Chinese ICBM may have a shorter range. It is capable of carrying 8-10 MRVs. The October 1993 nuclear testing in Lop Nor was that of a warhead for the MRV, estimated at 70-90kt.

The North Korean version of this strategic missile, the *NoDong-X*, is a vast technological improvement over the *NoDong* and *TaepoDong* SSMs. In its development, the DPRK also utilized the latest Russian-Soviet technology obtained from numerous Russian engineers and technicians working in North Korea. Consequently, the *NoDong-X* achieved an extension of range and greater power through miniaturization of the warhead and adaptation of solid fuel. The anticipated range of the *NoDong-X* in its initial version is over 6,000 km. **This means the DPRK's *NoDong-X* missile is intercontinental and can hit parts of the continental US**. The Russian assessment is that the *NoDong-X* is "a long-range assault weapon." ROK's Deputy Prime Minister Yi Yong-Tok also called the *NoDong-X* "a strategic weapon." Considering the intensity of the development work in the PRC and the DPRK, the *NoDong-X* may be operational as soon as 1996-97.

13

THE DEVELOPMENT OF NUCLEAR WEAPONS

The North Korean nuclear program can be traced back to the 1950s, when Kim Il-Song sought to balance the presence of US nuclear weapons in South Korea. At first, the DPRK's program was only a minor part of the regional socialist nuclear umbrella provided by the USSR and the PRC. Indeed both countries provided the DPRK with its first nuclear facilities and the training of its scientists and experts. But Pyongyang's commitment to the development of nuclear weapons grew markedly in the 1960s and even more so in the mid to late 1970s. Kim Jong-Il, Kim Il-Song's son and heir, was put directly in charge of the fledgling nuclear program, reflecting the extent of Pyongyang's commitment to becoming a nuclear power.

The development of nuclear weapons had a direct and immediate impact on the KPA. According to KPA Capt. Shin Chung-Chol, since 1980, KPA officers at the Kim Il-Song Military Academy, the DPRK's highest military institution, "attended a lecture on the 'offensive with nuclear attacks' in the tactics course in the college." Capt. Shin stressed that "the lecture was given in anticipation of North Korea's nuclear attacks against enemies." In early 1994, he added that considering the emphasis put on nuclear warfare among the KPA's elite officers already in the early 1980s, "there is no doubt that North Korea has nuclear weapons."

A crash program of building nuclear facilities for military use began in 1980. The emphasis was on self-sufficiency in both raw materials and basic technologies. Significantly, the North Korean nuclear reactor technology was based on proven US and British models of the 1950s and not an expansion of the Soviet-Chinese reactor technologies already available to the DPRK. In September 1980, the DPRK began construction on a 30mw gas cooled reactor, a configuration extremely efficient for producing Plutonium. Construction was largely completed in 1984, and the reactor was activated in February 1987. The US-educated Prof. Kyong Won Ha is one of the key scientists and engineers behind the 30mw reactor in Yongbyon.

In 1984, the DPRK began the construction of a major new military nuclear complex in the Yongbyon area built around a new reactor in the 50-200mw range dedicated for weapons production. Construction was near completion in 1989 and the reactor was expected to be activated in 1992. The construction of auxilliary installations for this reactor was expected to be completed in 1994 in the aftermath of a crash program begun in 1993. Within two years after its activation, now expected to take place in 1995 at the latest, this reactor alone will be producing enough Plutonium for 10-12 weapons a year.

As of late-1991, the DPRK began digging deep tunnels near Yongbyon to shield and conceal the key components of its military nuclear program. A new air defense system was deployed in November 1991, and above-ground facilities are being hardened. Meanwhile, a prototype reprocessing facility was completed in 1987 and is producing some 15kgs of plutonium annually. The work on a reprocessing facility for nuclear fuels began around 1988 and is expected to become operational around 1994. The clandestine plutonium factory for the nuclear weapons, which is called by the DPRK "radiological laboratory," is a single-story building constructed on top of the main plutonium reprocessing facility now buried underground. Meanwhile, since mid 1993, the DPRK has doubled its capacity to produce Plutonium by installing a second production line in the main reprocessing facility.

Moreover, the DPRK also built highly secret underground facilities in Pakchon. Since underground facilities are extremely difficult to construct, the mere fact the DPRK has committed itself to underground military nuclear facilities reflects self-confidence in its technological capabilities.

The initial success of the nuclear construction programs was not sufficient to have a strategic impact. In the mid-1980s, it was the combination of Pyongyang's increased commitment to an anti-US confrontational strategy, and its access to Iranian-Western-educated scientists and Libyan clandestine procurement of high technology that convinced Pyongyang to significantly expand its military nuclear program even before the initial phase was complete. Ko Yong-Hwan, a recent high level defector, explained that the highest levels in Pyongyang concluded around 1985 that they "cannot cope with the situation with conventional weapons; therefore nuclear weapons must be developed [as] the last means for preserving their political system." In January 1986, Kim Il-Song alluded to Pyongyang's decision by introducing the imminence of a US nuclear threat to the DPRK. "Today the greatest danger of nuclear war hovers over the Korean peninsula," he explained. As a direct result of the US military activities, "South Korea has become the most dangerous hotbed of nuclear war, and our country is in a critical situation where war may break out any minute."

One reason for the DPRK's confidence is the sudden access to Western nuclear technology, mainly West German, made possible in the mid-1980s through the strategic cooperation of the DPRK, Libya, Syria, and Iran. Ko Yong-Hwan confirmed that the North Korean nuclear program utilized diversified technology from West European sources. Indeed, the DPRK's new 50mw research reactor, built near the submarine base in Sinpo, is German-made. Like the Yongbyon complex, the Sinpo reactor is the center of a large scale underground complex. Simultaneously, in May 1989, the DPRK and the GDR (East Germany) signed a comprehensive agreement on the transfer of "substantial" amounts of German nuclear technology and nuclear weapons materials, including enriched uranium, to Pyongyang.

Another indication of the sudden acceleration and expansion of the North Korean nuclear program was the sudden increase in the need for nuclear materials.

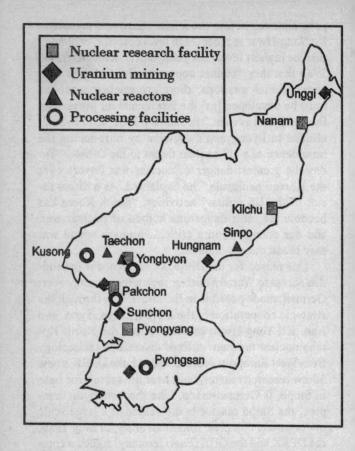

Fig 14 — The nuclear sites in North Korea. Note the concentration of facilities near the Pyongyang-Yongbyon zone. The exact location of several clandestine sites near the Chinese border is not known.

Fig 15 — A closer look at the Yongbyon area, the heart of the North Korean military nuclear effort. Note the diversity of the installations and their rapid expansion. KEY: Y-Yongbyon; K-Kunon River; 1-Russian reactors; 2-Support and housing facilities; 3-Research center; 4-Nuclear power plant; 5-Building 500; 6-Nuclear fuel fabrication center and research site; 7-Nuclear reprocessing plant, receiving and storage site; 8-New waste site; 9-Old waste site; 10-Construction site for nuclear facilities and test site; 11-30mw reactor; 12-Airbase; 13-Garrison; 14- 50-200mw reactor; 15-Construction of new "radiological laboratory."

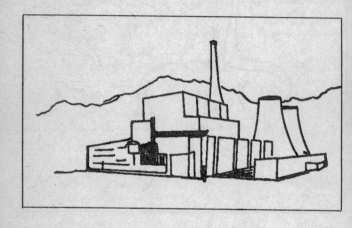

Fig 16 — The DPRK's nuclear facility in Yongbyon. Ostensibely
a power-generating reactor, there are no electrical wires leading from the site, nor are there any transformer stations in the
vicinity. This indicates that the reactor is used for pure nuclear
activities, mainly the generation of bomb material.

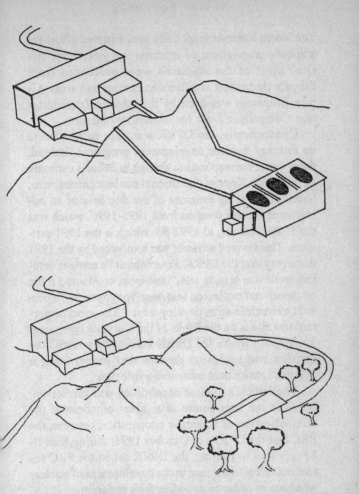

Fig 17 — An example of the North Korean effort to subvert the
IAEA inspections of their nuclear facilities. In 1989, a distinct
nuclear waste treatment facility could be seen (top). By 1992,
the building and the pipes leading to it from the main nuclear
reprocessing plant were completely buried underground. An
arms warehouse was built on top the waste site, and trees
planted around the site (bottom).

The North Koreans launched a concentrated effort for a speedy acquisition of uranium and cobalt via Africa. Most of the materials were purchased from Libya's traditional suppliers in central and west Africa. Shipment was done by the African Transportation Company, a front for Libyan intelligence.

Consequently, the DPRK was able to accelerate its military nuclear development programs. Indeed, there was a corresponding change in Seoul's estimate of the North Korean operational nuclear capabilities. Seoul changed its estimate of the due date of an operational nuclear weapon from 1995-1996, which was the 1989 estimate, to 1992-93, which is the 1991 estimate. This revised estimate was reinforced by the 1991 discovery that the DPRK already built "a nuclear detonation device testing site," and even conducted a big conventional explosion test near Yongbyon as "a prelude to nuclear arms development." The most important test site is on the banks of the Kuryong river, near Yongbyon , where the DPRK successfully tested the ignition and explosion devices that propel nuclear charges into critical mass and explosion.

The DPRK's nuclear capabilities will further improve in the near future as a direct outcome of the intensification of scientific cooperation between the PRC and the DPRK. In October 1991, during Kim Il-Song's visit to Beijing, the DPRK asked the PRC for technological assistance in the development of nuclear weapons in order to expedite their program.

By now, North Korea was already a nuclear power. A KGB document of 22 February, 1990, asserts that the DPRK had nuclear weapons as of early-1990. Kim Jong-Il "personally controls" the DPRK's military nuclear program that is aimed at "achieving military superiority over South Korea" as well as realizing "the prestigious aim of becoming one of the states possessing such weapons." The KGB reported that "development of the first atomic explosive device has been completed at the DPRK Center for Nuclear Research, located in the city of Yenben [Yongbyon]," and that "there are no plans to test it, in the interest of concealing from world opinion and from the controlling international organizations the actual fact of the production of nuclear weapons in the DPRK."

The KGB's comment concerning the North Korean decision not to test their nuclear weapons is important because it came just after Moscow rejected repeated requests by Pyongyang to test their nuclear weapons in the Soviet underground testing site in Kazakhstan. Pyongyang insisted that such a test be conducted and reported as a Soviet nuclear test so as to shield and conceal the DPRK's obtaining of nuclear weapons. Yi Chung-Kuk, a Sergeant in a chemical-warfare unit who defected in mid March 1994, disclosed that since 1991 he had "heard on several occasions ... from high-ranking military cadres and his senior officers that North Korea has already completed nuclear weapons development." Moreover, another defector who reached South Korea in December 1993 swore that he had "helped dig a tunnel to store nuclear materiel more than five years ago," that is, in the late 1980s.

In 1992, the DPRK began activating the purely military component of its nuclear program, essentially the weapon assembly. Since June 1992, there have been intensified activities in the DPRK's primary nuclear weapons site, an elaborate underground complex called Building 500, at Yongbyon. Activities there have included fortification, extensive camouflage and deployment of defenses, including new SA-2 batteries. As of late 1992, the extent of activities in and around the building increased to such an extent that it was impossible not to detect the military use of Building 500. Indeed, the DPRK announced its withdrawal from the NPT once the IAEA inspectors requested access to Building 500. Furthermore, in the spring of 1993, on the eve of the crisis over the North Korean nuclear effort, the KPA quickly established 40 military encampments, three airbases, a major ammunition depot, and deployed some 300 heavy anti-aircraft guns around the Yongbyon complex. During 1993, the KPA conducted 21 air defense drills at the complex, compared with four in the entire 1992. All of these activities clearly reflect Pyongyang's determination to fight for its military nuclear capabilities.

In mid 1993, the DPRK had about six nuclear weapons in operational status. At the very least, the DPRK has already "virtually completed" these six nuclear bombs and they are currently stored at "laboratory nuclear devices" status. The DPRK will have its nuclear-tipped 1,500km SSM operational by 1996-7. These 1993 reports are consistent with the above cited KGB report of February 1990 which stated that the DPRK had already completed the development of its "first atomic explosive device." These 1993 reports also reaffirm the late 1991 reports based on material provided by high-level North Korean defectors that the DPRK would be able to produce three to five "small nuclear bombs" a year by 1993.

In the last days of May 1993, the DPRK conducted an intense test launching program of all its ballistic missiles including the basic NK-SCUD-B, the NK-

SCUD-C, and the *NoDong-1*. Four missiles were launched in quick succession into a section of the Sea of Japan between the Korean coast and a point some 350km off Noto Peninsula in central Japan. In the spring of 1993, the Iranians took delivery of a few models of a follow-up to the *NoDong-1* modified for "delivering nuclear warheads" with a range of 1300km. With the 1,500-2,000km *NoDong-2*, the DPRK would be able threaten Tokyo, Beijing, and Vladivostok with nuclear strikes, a major strategic posture with global ramifications. Indeed, according to a former KPA officer who defected in the fall of 1992, it is common knowledge among the elite units of the KPA that their country has nuclear weapons and that their missiles "could destroy even Japan, the United States, or South Korea."

In order to confirm the status of the North Korean military nuclear capabilities, a high level delegation of West European diplomats and experts based in Beijing visited the DPRK in the early winter of 1993. Returning from Pyongyang in mid December, the delegation reported that the DPRK has "several atomic bombs and the vehicles to launch them." The delegation confirmed much of the data provided by defectors, including that North Korea "has built several kilo-size bombs. We established as well that testing sites exist." On the basis of the DPRK's verified plutonium production, the delegation concluded that the DPRK already has "at least half a dozen bombs." The delegation also confirmed that all the North Korean ballistic missiles, namely the NK-SCUD-B, NK-SCUD-C and the *NoDong-1*, have been adapted as platforms for nuclear warheads and are being mass produced. Before the end of 1993, the DPRK had already produced over 120 operational *NoDong-1* SSMs.

Most of the North Korean nuclear weapons are 50kt warheads for the ballistic missiles, each weighing around 500kg. These warheads are being readied for launch. Yim Yong-Son, a KPA 1st. Lt. who defected recently, reported that the special tank unit in Ambyon, Kangwon province, "has a separate steel container that can store nuclear bombs during war time." These weapons will be delivered to the front as needed. In late January 1994, a highly informed Chinese official reported that he had "recently heard from a senior North Korean official that North Korea is hiding nuclear weapons in an underground warehouse in the mountains near Pyongyang and that any thorough inspection of North Korean nuclear facilities by the United States will fail to locate them." Yi Chung-Kuk also learned from his senior officer that "it will be of no use to inspect Yongbyon because nuclear weapons are being produced at another place." Nevertheless, in early 1994, the KPA resumed building fortifications as well as strengthening numerous underground facilities in the Yongbyon area. The pace of work as well as the numerous defensive exercises conducted in the area strongly suggest an anticipation of war.

Furthermore, there are indications and defector reports that the North Korean nuclear arsenal may be bigger than the six weapons estimated. According to fairly well-confirmed reports, the DPRK succeeded in smuggling 56kg. of plutonium from the CIS (former Soviet Union) in early 1992. This plutonium is sufficient for the production of 10 additional warheads, the first of which was expected to be completed in the spring of 1993. The work on these warheads is continuing away from the rest of the North Korean nuclear program. In the fall of 1993, a defector reported the existence of "a dreadful underground nuclear plant in the Chagang-Do province in the northern area" where the most sensitive weapons-related activities take place. Isolated in the mountains near the Chinese border, this facility has relatively easy access to the roads and railway from Siberia. This simplifies the transfer of nuclear material from Russia.

Meanwhile, the DPRK continues to expand its already large nuclear infrastructure. By late 1993, some 20 facilities related to nuclear development were identified and there are not yet fully confirmed reports about several other facilities. Very telling is the ongoing construction of large scale reactors, such as the 200mw reactor in Taechon and the 635mw reactor in Sinpo. Ostensibly built as commercial-purpose reactors, these are old-type graphite-moderated and gas-cooled reactors that are relatively unsafe and their efficiency is relatively low when compared to more modern technologies long used in the West. However, reactors of this design produce extremely large quantities of plutonium, the key ingredient in nuclear weapons, as a by product of their activities even with natural, low-quality uranium. Thus, the reactor building program of the DPRK testifies to Pyongyang's commitment to markedly expand its nuclear weapons program in the very near future. The large reactors are expected to become "hot" in the next few years.

14

THE HIGH COMMAND OF THE CURRENT KPA

The last phase of the modernization of the KPA has been dominated by the knowledge that the DPRK was about to have nuclear weapons. The nuclear weapons factor has had a direct influence on the assertiveness and self confidence of the KPA build-up and the evolution of its perception of a future war. It is noteworthy that after acquiring nuclear technology, the revised KPA deployment of their non-nuclear weapons indicated the availability of nuclear weapons as a back-up.

As the KPA was putting the finishing touches on the acquisition of a new generation of weapon systems required to meet the challenges of the contemporary battlefield, the operational concepts for the future battlefield were being studied. The North Korean High Command anticipated a high-intensity battlefield in which the use of long-range ballistic missiles and strike aircraft, as well as chemical, biological and even nuclear weapons, would be viable options. Active preparations began in earnest.

Most important was the re-organization of the higher-level command and strategic weapons activated on the basis of a political decision. The proposal of a method of command was the first major military related action undertaken by Kim Jong-Il, then already increasingly involved in overseeing the development of nuclear weapons.

In the spring of 1983, Kim Jong-Il introduced the "3-channel 3-day reports". The "3-channel 3-day reports" was a new centralized command and control system aimed at ensuring civilian control over the new strategic capabilities at the disposal of the KPA. The program was launched once it became clear to Kim Jong-Il that the nuclear program was on the right track and that within a foreseeable time the DPRK would have nuclear capabilities.

The primary outcome of Kim Jong-Il's "3-channel 3-day reports" method was to ensure that Kim Jong-Il received accurate reports on every minor event in the KPA. The term "3 channels" means three channels of reporting, each independent from the others to ensure objectivity and independent confirmation of reported data. These channels are: 1. via the political department; 2. via the military staff; and 3. via the command structure. The term "3 days" means that all planning, decision making, and reporting of anticipated actions should take place and reported 3 days before they are to be implemented. These actions include: 1. movements of troop bodies larger than a platoon outside the area of responsibility of the division; 2. movement of any tank, armored vehicle, or other types of heavy weapons outside their district; 3. the movement of any fire weapon, from mortars to artillery to SSMs, outside their district.

In reality, this method of reporting is still in effect today and includes the movement of all weapon systems within the districts themselves. Reportedly, Kim Jong-Il's supervisory staff is very meticulous in studying the details of the reports and issues repeated requests for clarification and explanations in case of the smallest discrepancy between the various reports.

In the late 1980s, there was a further modification of the decision-making process. In the event of a major war, answering directly to Kim Il-Song and Kim Jong-Il will be the General Staff with the Chief of the General Staff acting as the main professional military commander. At present, Marshal O Chin-U, the closest confidant of Kim Il-Song and the Minister of Defense, is holding this position. (The Chief of General Staff, Choe Kwang, is in a peculiar position as shall be discussed below.)

Marshal O Chin-U (b. 1910) is one of the founding fathers of the DPRK's military system. A legendary partisan since 1935, he fought with Kim Il-Song in Manchuria and returned together with him to Korea. From the very beginning, he held several sensitive and important positions such as preparing special forces for the subversion of South Korea. O Chin-U steadily rose in rank due to his rare combination of professional excellence and complete devotion to Kim Il-Song. During the Korean War, he served as the commander of III Corps. In the mid 1950s, he served as the Chief of Staff of the Air Force.

O Chin-U was promoted to full general in 1964. Soon afterwards, he became active politically, playing central roles in the purges of Kim Il-Song's victims. In 1976 he was nominated Minister of Defense, a post he currently holds. O Chin-U, was promoted to Vice-Marshal in 1985, and became, at that time, second in rank only to Kim Il-Song. Although the KPA is in the most dynamic reform and modernization process in its history, in October 1990, O Chin-U wrote an article highlighting the lasting importance of the early partisan struggle led by Kim Il-Song to the development and success of the DPRK and WPK. O Chin-U is considered number three in the hierarchy of the DPRK. In case of the sudden death of Kim Il-Song, O Chin-U is believed to actively support the succession of Kim Jong-Il, if only out of devotion to the father.

Although Marshal O Chin-U has been the primary beneficiary of the marked rise in the power of the position of Chief of the General Staff, the real military brain behind the revolutionary modernization of the KPA was General O Kuk-Yol. Although seemingly out of sight, O Kuk-Yol is still one of the most important senior military figures in the DPRK. From a strategic military point of view, the nuclearization of the DPRK's military system is the work of General O Kuk-Yol.

General O Kuk-Yol is the military confidant and right-hand man of Kim Jong-Il. What O Chin-U is to Kim Il-Song, O Kuk-Yol is to Kim Jong-Il. It is also noteworthy that O Kuk-Yol and O Chin-U, are distant relatives.

The son of a legendary partisan who was killed fighting alongside Kim Il-Song in the 1930s, O Kuk-Yol is a graduate of prestigious party schools, including the Mangyongdae specialized elementary school system for orphans of DPRK's wars, in which children of the WPK's elite also enroll. He then had a brilliant military career, including studies in the Frunze Academy and other key military schools in the USSR. In the 1970s and 1980s, he was the Chief of the General Staff. In this capacity, he "played a vanguard role in the military in laying the ground work for the hereditary succession of power by Kim Jong-Il." At this stage he became Kim Jong-Il's confidant. The most important military reforms since the 1950s were conducted under O Kuk-Yol, then Chief of the General Staff, in the mid 1980s. O Kuk-Yol was then "regarded as Kim Jong-Il's right hand man." (At that time Kim Jong-Il became personally responsible for, and in charge of, the DPRK's military nuclear program.)

O Kuk-Yol was suddenly dismissed in February 1988, ostensibly purged, and appointed the commander of the DPRK's Civil Defense. However, a defector disclosed that the appointment was "due to policy consideration because he was not well acquainted with that field." In reality, O Kuk-Yol was sent to study principles of nuclear warfare so he can make decisions during Kim Jong-Il's ascendancy. Indeed, in April 1990, O Kuk-Yol participated in the 9th Supreme People's Assembly Session, conclusively proving that he had not been purged. Soon afterwards, another defector from the North Korean military predicted that "O Kuk-Yol will stage a comeback in 2-3 years," or by the time Kim Jong-Il assumes full power. This observation proved very accurate due to the fact that O Kuk-Yol re-emerged into a uniquely senior post in mid 1993.

Under the current system of command and control, the KPA's Chief of the General Staff, Choe Kwang, holds tremendous power over the conduct of the war. Recent reorganization further increased the power of the Chief of the General Staff. All corps commands and separate commands (such as air force and navy) are directly answerable to him. This assignment marks the tightening of centralized command. The General Staff increased their control over the entire armed forces, especially such high performance combat arms as the navy and air force. These were now integrated into the command and control system of a General Staff dominated by the army. Indeed, during wartime, the navy and air force in effect have no staff of their own. At the end of the modification process, the KPA was organized very much like the PRC's PLA in the aftermath of its nuclearization process.

The KPA Chief of the General Staff, Marshal Choe Kwang, is a rising political-military force in the DPRK. Choe Kwang is another veteran partisan who had fought along with Kim Il-Song since 1935, but then returned to Pyongyang with an advance Soviet unit on 15 August 1945 (Kim Il-Song did not reenter Korea until 19 September 1945). A devotee of Kim Il-Song, he played a central role in the organization of the KPA. During the Korean War, Choe Kwang distinguished himself as a division commander at the front. After the war, he served as the commander of the Kanggon Military Academy, and then as a vice Minister of Defense. In 1963, Choe Kwang was nominated the Chief of the General Staff and began a quick climb in the political hierarchy as well, only to be suddenly dismissed and seemingly purged in 1969.

In the late 1970s, Choe Kwang began a slow climb back, and in late 1980 was back at the fringes of the top leadership in Pyongyang. His rise was attributed to a maneuver by Kim Il-Song to ensure that all emerging old leaders are "conservative hard-liners of the partisan faction." The marked rise of O Chin-U and Choe Kwang was the most explicit aspect of this power maneuver.

Then, in February 1988, Choe Kwang, a Kim Il-Song devotee, was suddenly promoted and nominated Chief of the General Staff instead of the dismissed O Kuk-Yol. Kim Il-Song selected this veteran professional to oversee a most important transformation of the DPRK Armed Forces. However, while in office, Choe Kwang proved himself as "a key supporter of Kim Jong-Il". Indeed, Choe Kwang has been doing his utmost to strengthen the military system for the impending succession of power.

Ultimately, however, the re appointment of Choe Kwang as Chief of the General Staff was primarily a decision based on professional considerations. Choe Kwang is known as "a believer in weapons" and "an expert on modern warfare." He is often described as "a man absolutely fixated on weapons and as such is a specialist with a keen understanding of modern warfare." Choe Kwang was the motivating force behind North Korea's acquisition and production of new weapons, the foundation upon which Pyongyang has modernized its military. Choe Kwang had his ups and downs in the political hierarchy. In May 1990, the power of Choe Kwang, as the Chief of the General Staff, was rising in comparison with that of O Chin-U, the veteran Minister of Defense. It is noteworthy that the elevation in the political position of Choe Kwang was primarily an expression of the growing importance of his position and not just the individual.

In mid February 1990, a key report was published in Pyongyang, detailing a five-point "programmatic guideline...to strengthen the People's Army." issued by Kim Il-Song. The program "represents an application of the principles of *Juche* ideology in the building of revolutionary armed forces, based on a scientific analysis of the requirements of modern warfare." Alluding to the acquisition of nuclear weapons, Pyongyang reported that "the KPA came to posses a powerful compass for fighting against whatever enemy it may confront and winning over him."

This next milestone of the DPRK's modernization of military doctrine took place in mid February 1990, just about the time the DPRK obtained its first nuclear device. It is noteworthy that the principles of this reform were published in Pyongyang only a few days before the KGB confirmed that North Korea had finished building its "atomic explosive device."

After the customary rendition of the importance of "revolutionary spirit" and related slogans, the expertise of the KPA was stressed stronger than ever before. "The political and ideological superiority of a revolutionary army becomes truly powerful when it is combined with a high level of military skill." The report then went on to stress the crucial importance of modern warfare involving high technology and sophisticated weapons systems. "Modern warfare is scientific warfare in which the high achievements of science and technology are directly introduced; mechanized warfare in which modern arms and equipment are massively mobilized; and three-dimensional warfare in which fighting takes places in the air, on the ground, in the sea, on the front-line and in the rear."

Almost immediately, there followed a distinct increase in the overall militarism of the Pyongyang media. There was a preoccupation with the reunification of the Korean peninsula by military means. Novel, however, was the emphasis that the military duties, up to and including the liberation of South Korea, were meant to protect Kim Il-Song and his Korea. "This means that the military service is essentially a process of revolutionary struggle to protect the safety of our Great Leader and uphold by arms the ideology and intent of our leader and Comrade Leader. Our people's army is the army of our leader, the army of the party, the fundamental mission of which is to protect and defend our Great Leader and dear Comrade Leader by arms." Pyongyang emphasized that the only true and complete defense of both Kim Il-Song and Kim Jong-Il, and their Pyongyang was by the eradication of any challenge, especially from the ROK: "The struggle to ensure national reunification is, precisely, the most honorable task assigned the youth of our times who are destined to represent the new generation of our revolution."

In late May 1990, in the 9th Supreme People's Assembly Session, the DPRK established the National Defense Commission of the DPRK with Kim Il-Song as chairman, Kim Jong-Il as first vice-chairman, O Chin-U and Choe Kwang as vice-chairmen, and 7 other members. It was a major step in the militarization of the nation, if more could be done. These steps were adopted in the context of Kim Il-Song's observation that "establishing the party's monolithic ideological system is the main guarantee for the organizational and ideological consolidation of its ranks."

From a strategic point of view, the establishment of the National Defense Commission of the DPRK is a most important event. It further solidified Kim Jong-Il's hold over power. Moreover, it clearly identified the dominant aspect of Pyongyang's policy and decision making. The powers of the Committee are constantly being expanded. Beyond O Chin-U and Choe Kwang, the other seven members are active and semi-retired senior officers. The Commission positions Kim Jong-Il "to direct the first generation of revolutionaries," to date personally answerable only to Kim Il-Song. The new appointment thus underscores the strength of Kim Jong-Il's influence in the KPA, despite the mistrust of several professional senior officers. Thus, the politicization of the high command significantly strengthened Kim Jong-Il's position with it.

By now, the structure of the DPRK High Command was settled. The supreme authority is still a combination of Kim Il-Song with Kim Jong-Il, with the latter increasingly assuming the leadership position. This was clearly demonstrated in the "Semi-War State" declared by Kim Jong-Il in the spring of 1993 (to be discussed below). The new National Defense Council operates under the supreme leader in an advisory and professional assistance capacity. The Council seems to have taken over some of the main responsibilities of the WPK's Military Commission, but not replaced it completely. The primary mission of the National Defense Council is to serve as a sounding board and collective conscience for cases of total war and anticipated huge casualties and destruction. For the actual conduct of the war, the even more powerful General Staff is the sole agency responsible for actual military operations. Under the General Staff there are 14 bureaus:

1. Operations Bureau, responsible for all overt military operations and covert actions (intelligence,

special operations, subversion activities) in the Korean peninsula and world wide.

2. Military Training Bureau, responsible for training of the standing army, the vast reserve system, school children, etc.

3. Military Mobilization Bureau, in charge of the mobilization of the entire country, the militarization of infrastructure, call-up of draftees and reservists, as well as allocation of national assets to military construction projects.

4. Weapons Bureau, in charge of weapons development and production.

5. Enlisted Personnel Bureau, responsible for personnel matters of enlistment from handling of recruitment (of individuals) to soldiers' quality of life, education, etc.

6. Classified Documents Bureau, responsible for counter intelligence and internal security of all paperwork, as well as encryption matters, and communications security.

7. Reconnaissance Bureau, in effect military intelligence, responsible for collection of intelligence world wide, threat analysis, as well as the running of special forces, covert actions world wide, and international terrorism. Such forces as the Special 8th Corps (Special Forces), and Units 907, 198, 448 (terrorism) answer to the Bureau.

8. Military Engineer Bureau, In charge of constructing facilities for military uses, combat engineering services in war and peace, and mining activities.

9. Cadre Personnel Bureau, responsible for personnel matters of officers from handling of recruitment, promotions and advances, to the quality of life, education, etc. of the officers and their families. The

Bureau handles predominantly professional issues rather than political.

10. Telecommunications Bureau, in charge of running the nation's electronic communication system, from telephones to radio, as well as monitoring (technically) other people's communication traffic.

11. Geological Bureau, in charge of research of terrain, weather, topography, mapping, weather forecast, and selection of sites for deep digging of underground facilities, tunnels, bunkers, etc.

12. Inspection Bureau, the inspector general who is responsible for all supervisory work.

13. Military Publication Bureau, publishes all military material, from highly classified textbooks and war plans, to a host of manuals, periodicals, propaganda leaflets, etc. Also responsible for books for the military universities and schools.

14. Rear Area Services Bureau, a unique entity that has the undisputed overriding authority for the day-to-day management of the nation's so-called civilian infrastructure and virtually all aspects of life in North Korea so that they are constantly ready to contribute to the military build-up and war effort. In essence, this Bureau controls all the means of transportation, food production, medical services, clothing manufacturing, construction, maintenance, veterinary services, the financial system, industrial infrastructure, and every other productive aspect of society. There is hardly anything in North Korea that does not fall under the responsibility and authority of the Rear Area Services Bureau. The Bureau is always of greater power and authority than the civilian organizations ostensibly and nominally responsible for these functions of civilian and everyday life in the DPRK.

Separate and equally powerful is the General Political Affairs Bureau. It is an all-powerful and separate entity of the KPA, which is completely independent of the KPA High Command. The Bureau answers directly to the WPK, functioning solely through the WPK's Military Commission, and then to Kim Il-Song and Kim Jong-Il. The General Political Affairs Bureau runs the entire political educational supervisory system of the KPA, ensuring that all their activities are politically correct. The Bureau's officers are fiercely loyal to both Kim Il-Song and Kim Jong-Il. They constitute the source of the propaganda, education, agitation, and personality cult material. They control not just the souls of soldiers but all North Koreans who might be required to contribute to the war effort, in essence every single North Korean. The main components of the General Political Affairs Bureau are:

1. Organizational and Planning Division
2. Party Organization Division
3. Socialist Youth League Guidance Division
4. Propaganda and Education Division
5. Cultural Division
6. Special Political Division
7. Inspection Division
8. Information Division
9. Cadre Division
10. Special Operation Division (a.k.a. Unit 563), responsible for subversion of South Korea, inducing defections, spreading propaganda and misinformation.
11. Publishing Corps
12. Army's Newspaper Corps
13. The 2-8 Film Studio
14. The 2-8 Athletic Corps

15. The Army's Concert Corps

The elaborate, powerful, and professionally competent system of High Command is not only tightly controlled by Kim Il-Song and Kim Jong-Il, but also stresses its loyalty to the individuals themselves rather than to the government and Party positions they hold. Under this elaborate system of High Command comes the most militarized and tightly controlled state on earth, the People's Republic of Korea. It is, in effect, a state built to serve the needs of the Korean People's Army. In turn, the sole purpose of the KPA is to unify the Korean peninsula by force of arms. All of these preparations and sacrifices are carried out in order to satisfy the manifest destiny of the Great Leader and his son and heir, the Dear Leader.

15

THE PRESENT DAY KPA

The organization and structure of the KPA is derived from the military structure of the USSR. The main offensive units of the KPA, as well as their basic operational art and tactics, have undergone tremendous qualitative improvements on the basis of a flow of Soviet military expertise and advice since the mid-1980s. The KPA, both the standing army and the vast reserve-mobilization assets, are controlled via a peacetime organization that can transform itself literally overnight into a wartime system. As will be discussed below, certain key components of the KPA remain on a wartime footing at all time, thus greatly enhancing the DPRK's ability to launch a surprise attack at any moment.

Under the General Staff, the KPA is divided into two main segments:

1. Eight Corps, which are, like the Military Districts in the USSR, peacetime territory administration and force maintenance bodies with wartime headquarters.

2. Several dedicated units that are constantly in war fighting status. These are: one Special Corps (Special Forces), the Navy, Air Force, artillery, mechanized forces, guided missiles, and the Capital Defense Command.

All of the dedicated units are directly subordinated to the General Staff and all communications and coordination between them and the various Corps headquarters in whose territory they are stationed take place via the General Staff to ensure tight control. (see fig.18)

The main ground units of the KPA, those under the control of the eight corps, are divided into "commitment units" which are deployed in the "forward" regions along the DMZ, and the "reserve units" deployed elsewhere to follow up and reinforce an advance. These standing units of the entire KPA are deployed in three echelons for gradual commitment to battle and replenishment of main thrusts and operations. The 3 echelons are:

1. The "forward" zone along the DMZ (W-to-E: IV Corps, II Corps, V Corps, I Corps);

2. The "center" belt between Pyongyang and Wonsan (W-to-E: III Corps, VII Corps); and

3. The inner home belt, the area near the Chinese border (W-to-E: VIII Corps, VI Corps).

In the forward zone there are 20 divisions divided between four corps, as well as a multitude of brigades, support units, and an independent aviation brigade, for a total of well over 300,000. They belong, from east to west, to the I Corps, V Corps, II Corps, IV Corps. These forces are devoted in peacetime to defense and security. In addition, they engage constantly in the building (digging) of additional facilities and

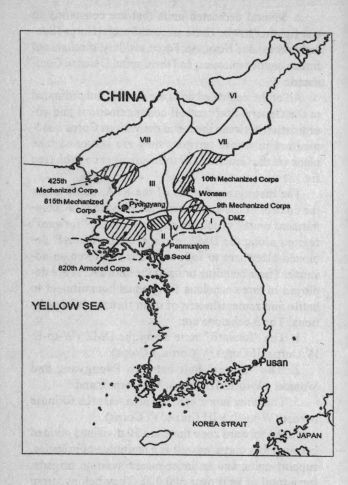

Fig 18 — The boundaries of the territorial corps of the KPA. Note that four of them, half the total, are along the DMZ.

bases. Virtually all weapons and company-size units are buried in specialized caves and underground shelters, and ready for assault by surprise. The troops of these corps also maintain the obstacle fields (from electric fences to unmarked mine fields) and other traps along the DMZ.

The forces of the central and rear areas divide their time between training and building. Some 100,000 troops are involved at any one time in construction projects. In cases of crash programs up to 200,000 and, in rare cases, even 300,000 troops can be mobilized for such activities. These troops come in addition to the full composition of the standing army so that their preoccupation with the construction work does not affect the readiness of the main units of the four corps. Moreover, all of these troops are trained as soldiers and in case of war will be assigned to the various engineering units. Thus, their daily activities have no impact whatsoever on the DPRK's ability to launch a surprise attack on the ROK. Meanwhile, as a direct result of the work of these troops, by 1991 most of the known military production and storage facilities in the DPRK were already fully protected, camouflaged and sheltered underground, with comprehensive air and civil/local defense systems deployed to protect the military production centers.

As a result of the recent reorganization of the armed forces, the KPA has significantly streamlined its ability to deploy the entire nation in an intense war scenario. The most important development was the selection of the corps as the primary offensive maneuver unit. The KPA believes that the corps is easy to control, move faster and is more flexible than the Mass Army, and, at the same time, sufficiently powerful to be able to implement the directives of the General Staff on its own.

Consequently, the eight corps commands, which previously had been only administrative and control bodies, were transformed into full-fledged headquarters that, in wartime, will lead main forces into combat. The eight corps currently control 35 infantry divisions, three mechanized-infantry divisions, two armored divisions, five armored brigades, four infantry brigades, two independent armored regiments, five independent infantry regiments, as well as all the mobilized forces that will be organized as infantry divisions.

This impressive force is but a component, albeit sizable, of a far larger military machine that in 1991 was the fifth largest army in the world, controlling over 1.2 million standing forces (1.1 million ground forces) and over five to six million reservists. In wartime, after 24-48 hours mobilization, the KPA would expand to the following size: 35 infantry divisions, three mechanized-infantry divisions, two armored divisions, one truck-mobile division, 26 reserve infantry divisions, 15 armored brigades, 23 mechanized brigades, four infantry brigades, 18 reserve infantry brigades, 22 special operations brigades, and a host of dedicated and specialized units and forces. Their Structure, under the General Staff, (see fig.19) is as follows:

* 820th Armored Corps
* Artillery Corps
* Capital Defense Corps
* Reconnaissance Bureau
* Air Force
* Navy

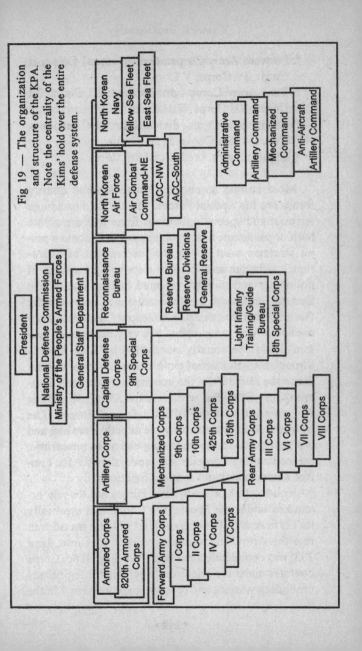

Fig 19 — The organization and structure of the KPA. Note the centrality of the Kims' hold over the entire defense system.

* Forward Army Corps , divided into: I Corps, II Corps, IV Corps, V Corps.
* Rear Army Corps , divided into: III Corps, VI Corps, VII Corps, VIII Corps
* Mechanized Corps , divided into: 9th Corps, 10th Corps, 425th Corps, 815th Corps
* Light Infantry, the Special 8th Corps.

Most unique among the North Korean quality forces are the Special Forces. The DPRK has a huge terrorist and special operations force that are active both in peacetime and are supposed to become a major strategic asset during the "sacred war of liberation." Although answering to a convoluted system of politically and military oriented bodies, mainly the General Staff itself, the Reconnaissance Bureau of the General Staff, and the WPK's Central Committee, they are actually all components of a very centralized system that is personally controlled by Kim Jong-Il through a small staff of experts fiercely loyal to him. Since the mid 1980s, the commander has been General Kang Chan Su, who took over from Kim Jung Rin, the father of the DPRK's Special Forces. The instructions for operations come directly from him and are sent down to the executing entity. In peacetime, the controlling agencies are predominantly for control-management and training functions.

The North Korean Special Forces are loosely organized under the Special 8th Corps, and especially its 124th Army. (The original Unit 124 was transferred into the Army, and another special forces unit, Unit 283, was completely absorbed.) The Special 8th Corps operates under the principle: "applying the legitimacy of modern warfare and revolutionary warfare." In the

8th Special Corps are four reconnaissance brigades (Units 60, 61, 62, and 63 of the Reconnaissance Bureau), eight light infantry brigades, 24 Special Forces brigades, three amphibious brigades, five air battalions, and two dedicated training centers (Units 907 & 198). According to a KPA Special Operations officer who defected in September 1993, these centers include a one-km long underground tunnel for infiltration training and full-size mock-ups of South Korean city streets, complete with shops displaying products made in South Korea.

In addition, the KPA has 35 Independent Light Infantry Battalions trained to operate on their own or on behalf of divisional forces. These battalions are sustained by five Elite Training Regiments (Units 90, 91, 92, 93, & 94), each equipped with its own tank and assault gun companies for training special force operations against heavy units. In wartime, these training units will be added to the elite forces. The Navy's special operations are controlled by Units 459, 632, 753, and 755 based on geographical location and intended landing sites along the ROK coast line. Units 217, 250, and many more oversee cross-DMZ infiltration by terrorist and reconnaissance detachments.

In addition, for politically sensitive and crucial operations, the DPRK relies on the Reconnaissance Bureau, which includes the high quality Special Purpose Forces (the KPA's version of the Soviet SPETSNAZ), and special sea-going units. The training of these SPETSNAZ troops is done by Unit 940 under the slogan "one against one hundred" and includes all types of armed and unarmed combat, sabotage, use of improvised instruments, as well as such unique skills as assassination with chop-sticks. A lot of training is conducted in US/ROK uniforms with enemy weapons and against full size mock-ups of specific targets built in the SPETSNAZ training centers. The training courses also include three years of English studies.

Furthermore, the DPRK has the separate Unit 695 of the political administration which is devoted to espionage and contacts with foreigners, including building underground groups and planting networks in the ROK, Japan and, increasingly, the US itself.

The DPRK fields highly lethal SPETSNAZ and terrorists throughout the Third World and even the US. North Korean intelligence operatives and Latin American terrorists receive advance and specialized training in Iran's Melli University. Since the 1970s, Japanese (many veteran JRA terrorists), Arabs, Central Americans and Puerto Ricans, and especially sub-Saharan Africans have been sent to the DPRK or Libya for recruitment and intensive training for intelligence work in their native countries. Within the United States, North Korean operatives are fully integrated into the Islamist terrorist movement and are expected to participate in their operations according to agreements reached between Tehran and Pyongyang.

Pyongyang has a specialized force for clandestine operations as instruments of state policy at the highest level under the Research Department for which Kim Jong-Il is personally responsible. Usually, he himself initiates and personally approves each and every special operation. The full name of this unique force is the Research Department for External Intelligence (RDEI). These forces carried out such operations as the October 1983 bombing attack in Rangoon on President Chun Doo Hwan and the entire South Korean government (killing 17 key officials and wounding several others including the president), and the November 1987 mid-air bombing of KAL flight 858 (killing 115 passengers). Kim Jong-Il is known to have approved both. According to Kim Hyun Hee (the perpetrator of the KAL operation) the whole mission was Kim Jong-Il's idea.

Meanwhile, the DPRK has been closely studying infiltration avenues into the US since early 1983, when four small North Korean freighters patrolled the coast of California and northern Mexico. Although their primary mission was to collect electronic intelligence, the ships were well equipped to conduct insertion operations. The Korean crews were members of the special forces also involved with Central American revolutionaries. Similar DPRK freighters had been used to insert the troops that attempted the assassination of the entire ROK government in Burma.

In mid 1993, in the aftermath of the "Semi-war state," the North Korean intelligence system underwent major changes that significantly increased their capabilities to operate in and against South Korea. The most important developement is that Gen. O Kuk-Yol, the military devotee of Kim Jong-Il, was nominated the Director of the Operations Department (a most important intelligence arm).

In this capacity, O Kuk-Yol first trained a whole new elite military force of ardent Party supporters, tailored after the troops of the Ministry of Interior in the USSR which include both regular and SPETSNAZ forces. The new North Korean units are trained to deal with domestic disturbances. They are Kim Jong-Il's Praetorian Guard.

However, it was not long before O Kuk-Yol

launched, under this cover, an intense program of highly sensitive spy and saboteur training for operations inside South Korea. These preparations are but a part, albeit an important one, of a major upgrading of the DPRK's terrorist and intelligence forces conducted by Kim Jong-Il to cope with forthcoming crises.

An Myong-Chin, an intelligence SPETSNAZ officer who defected in September 1993, disclosed that in the aftermath of these changes the DPRK intelligence is now known as "Office Complex No. 3." The main school and headquarters is known, since January 1992, as "The Kim Jong-Il Political and Military College" because of the growing importance of Kim Jong-Il to the intelligence system. The DPRK Intelligence Service is presently devided into four main departments with the following chiefs:

1. The Operations Department under Gen. O Kuk-Yol, responsible for all strategic covert military activities such as subversion, terrorism, and special operations.

2. The Social and Cultural Department, chief unknown, responsible for active measures and black propaganda.

3. The Reunification Front Department under Kang Chu-Il, which handles the unification fronts, student groups, and other subversive entities.

4. The External Information Investigation Department under Kwon Hui-Kyong, in charge of strategic espionage, military, political and economic intelligence, its analysis and presentation to the leadership.

All these Departments send operatives and spies into the ROK. Most important are the people of the Operations Department because in all operations they are always in charge of the illegal clandestine infiltration into South Korea, as well as the execution of the operations themselves inside the South, even when carried out by members of other departments. The Operations Department also has its own large force of SPETSNAZ and covert operatives—troops responsible for making certain key preparations for war. They organize and expand the sabotage and terrorist networks that will explode throughout rear areas of South Korea at the onset of war. All together, by mid 1993, the DPRK Intelligence already had over 1,000 such operatives, 200-300 of them were already operating inside South Korea. They were carrying out either espionage duties (in support of other departments) or active preparations for wartime activation.

The main intelligence school now has an eight km long South Korean city with restaurant, coffee shop, supermarket, stationery shop and other facilities. There the intelligence SPETSNAZ learn how to survive and operate clandestinely in the urban centers of the ROK. Despite the ideological threat of exposure to Western ideas, the school has a constant supply of the latest South Korean newspapers and movies. An Myong-Chin observed that the subway station and bus terminal, as well as some other key buildings in the intelligence school, are identical in every respect to those of Seoul.

Just how serious Pyongyang is about the imminence of hostilities and the key role of special operations in such a war can be learned from the training of the intelligence SPETSNAZ forces. Most important is the infiltration training of operatives of the Operations Department conducted by the "715 Laison Office." Training includes actual penetrations into

South Korea—through underground tunnels and other means. At times, the operatives stay a few kms south of the DMZ. An Myong-Chin reported that on several occasions he had penetrated more than 2 kms south of the DMZ in order to study and experiment with ROK and US military procedures, examine first hand the SPETSNAZ troops' ability to evade guards and patrols, and gain self-confidence.

There is independent confirmation of these defectors' reports. For example, on 6 March 1994, a ROK patrol discovered a few discarded weapons along the Imjin River, south of the DMZ. These weapons included a Soviet-made pistol, a US-made M-16, DPRK-made ammunition for both weapons, and German binoculars. These weapons were discarded one or two years ago, apparently by a DPRK SPETSNAZ team on an infiltration exercise.

Meanwhile, there are new indications of an impending escalation in North Korean special operations inside South Korea. Starting mid February 1994, there has been a marked increase in North Korean urgings for a popular uprising in the ROK. Pyongyang has launched an overt and covert propaganda blitz. For internal consumption, the DPRK media has been building anticipation of a popular uprising, including acts of revolutionary violence. Although presented as spontaneous actions by citizens of South Korea, these will actually be terrorist operations carried out by North Korean agents and operatives. The KPA is reminded anew of the DPRK's basic strategy of "revolution in South Korea first, unification of the fatherland second." Revolution means violence and terrorism induced by DPRK special operations troops.

Indeed, highly specialized assets were recently

activated in North Korea pending this anticipated escalation. Most important is a special commando unit in the Nampo Military and Political School comprised of 30 males and nine females. They are being prepared for imminent insertion into South Korea. All these operatives are orphans with no living relatives and were brought up, from infancy, in special institutes of the DPRK Intelligence. This upbringing instilled in them complete devotion to both Kim Il-Song and Kim Jong-Il, and an eagerness to commit acts of extreme bravery—even suicide operations—in the ROK. In early March 1994, some members of this unit, and numerous other comparable units, have already begun to secretly deploy into South Korea. These infiltration operations were still occurring at time of writing.

Ultimately, these changes in the DPRK Intelligence Service, and especially the Operations Department, are far more important than the mere escalation and intensification of their activities. The return of General O Kuk-Yol to the military and political forefront reverberates throughout the entire KPA. Despite his 1988 disappearence, O Kuk-Yol remains extremely popular among the KPA younger military cadres who are fiercely loyal to him. They are convinced, and not without reason, that he understands the challenges of modern warfare better than any other senior commander. He is also considered the soldiers' general. Little wonder, therefore, that O Kuk-Yol is widely expected to become the next Minister of the People's Armed Forces, either when Kim Jong-Il rises to power or, as long as Kim Il-Song remains at the helm, as soon as O Chin-U leaves office (retires willingly or dies). Until then, the mere knowledge that O Kuk-

Yol is back in a supreme post of responsibility and authority and is already rejuvenating the officer corps, is instilling in them additional confidence and resolve.

These qualities he is instilling will be needed by all KPA troops to meet the challenges presented by an armed invasion of the ROK.

For the main land offensive, the KPA has a rapidly expanding quality core consisting of the tank-oriented 820th Armored Corps, known in peacetime as the [supreme] Mechanized Headquarters, and the 4 Mechanized Corps (9th Corps, 10th Corps, 425th Corps, 815th Corps). The primary source of fire support is the Artillery Corps, known in peacetime as the Artillery Headquarters. (see fig.20)

The [supreme] Mechanized Headquarters trains all armored units in peacetime and leads the 820th Armored Corps in the event of war. There are four additional specialized Mechanized Headquarters, the 9th Corps, 10th Corps, 425th Corps, and 815th Corps. Each of these includes high-level staff under a junior general (discussed below).

The wartime 820th Armoured Corps is comprised of one armoured/tank division, one armoured/tank brigade, a tank repair station, and a tank pacification station to secure the general area where the unit is operating (including a mobile camp, logistical support facilities, and forces for self protection of the compound). An integral component of the Corps Headquarters in both peace and war is a tank school so the unit can constantly prepare new cadres in all levels to replenish losses. In peacetime, the school is attached to supreme headquarters nearby, where it remains in time of war even as the armoured units

Fig 20 — The routine deployment of the KPA's elite elements. note that these forces are deployed along the natural avenues of advance into South Korea and the ultimate encirclement of the entire peninsula.

advance into the depth of the enemy rear. The armoured tank division is composed of: a command section; a mechanised-infantry battalion; a tank regiment; a reconnaissance and special forces battalion; an artillery regiment; an anti-aircraft artillery battalion; a sapper battalion; a telecommunications battalion; a technical battalion; and a chemical company. The artillery regiment includes a fire control command unit, a gun/howitzer battalion, a mortar/MBRL battalion, and a technical battalion.

The Artillery Headquarters has two main fire missions—deep fire strike and air defense for maneuvering forces as they advance into enemy territory. The primary components are an anti-aircraft artillery division, an anti-aircraft artillery brigade, an anti-aircraft machine-gun brigade (for which most crews are female), and an independent anti-aircraft artillery regiment. In addition, Headquarters also controls the regular heavy artillery including one artillery battalion each of 122mm, 152mm, & 130mm gun/howitzers, 130mm coastal artillery, SCUD-type & FROG-type SSMs, as well as a special munitions control unit (responsible for handling weapons of mass destruction), and a weapons support unit. The Artillery Headquarters also has an artillery school to prepare new cadres at all levels to replace its losses. The school also controls simple weapons, such as 76.2mm & 122mm artillery battalions, mortar battalions, and the anti-tank reserve for self-defense.

The four Mechanized Corps (the 9th, 10th, 425th and 815th Corps) are the elite of the KPA's ground forces. In addition to them, eight territorial Corps are each forming at least one comparable mechanized unit to operate as their main strike force. The importance of the Mechanized Corps is evident from being commanded by a junior general. A Mechanized Corps is a task-oriented force whose specific composition changes according to the goal of each mission and available resources. It is usually comprised of three to four divisions, mechanized-infantry or armored depending on the mission, reinforced by independent brigades (infantry, rifle), artillery regiments, heavy mortar and rocket launcher regiments, anti-aircraft and anti-tank artillery regiments and battalions as needed. In addition, the corps operate telecommunication regiments, chemical battalions, balloon observation battalions, and military hospitals.

Despite the growing mechanization of the KPA, the follow-up forces are still organized as infantry corps. The infantry division is still the basic unit of the KPA as a whole. However, the infantry division is increasingly provided with specialist components such as self-propelled artillery and rocket launchers. Moreover, a chemical battalion is now attached to all maneuver units.

Since the late 1980s, the emphasis in the training of the KPA infantry units has been on mobilization, joint exercises, and quick mastering of the many new weapon systems. A growing emphasis is put on upgrading challenging maneuvers, lightening strikes, and deep penetration of rough terrain including flooded rice fields. Also, virtually all units undergo repeated training in operating under chemical contamination, and in the assault-crossing of rivers. Recently, the KPA constructed numerous obstacles and mock-ups of ROK DMZ-type defensive barriers in the main corps areas and KPA units repeatedly train in breaching these defense lines under realistic conditions of a surprise attack and deep offensive.

A new key unit of growing importance is the anti-tank mobile reserve. It is equipped with ATGMs, RPGs, sniper rifles, and anti-tank artillery. The KPA's lesson of the 1973 Yom Kippur War was that such units, if they are willing to absorb enormous casualties, can stop even the best tank forces through slow attrition. Therefore, virtually every unit in the KPA from brigade and division on upwards has its own anti-tank mobile reserve. Their objective is to neutralize and prevent enemy mobile or armored forces from interfering with the primary mission of the North Korean mother unit, namely to advance ceaselessly into the depth of the South's territory. Since these anti-tank blocking engagements are to be completed at all cost, suicidal operations are encouraged by the KPA High Command.

The vast majority of the KPA is made up of mobilized reserves in the form of infantry units, which are already being provided with some levels of motorization and mechanization, namely, an assortment of older hand-me-down equipment from the elite units. The entire population of the DPRK is prepared for mobilization and organized in four paramilitary organizations:

1. The Pacification Unit. Organized to form in 24 hours, it includes 26 infantry divisions and 18 infantry brigades that are highly trained and combat ready. These divisions are made of 20-30 year old reservists just released from military service. Their numbers are estimated at over 540,000-600,000 strong.

2. The Workers and Peasants Red Guards. Made up of every able bodied male citizen between the ages

of 15 and 45 who are not in the military or the Pacification Units, as well as all women between 18 and 30 years of age. In 24-48 hours, these reservists should be organized into local units guarding their immediate neighborhoods and places of work, including air-defense, construction, and communication missions. Then they would be further organized into fighting units as the need arises on the main front. Many are highly skilled workers in key production lines who are organized to defend their own factories and institutions (but would not be sent to the front). The Red Guards exceed 3,500,000-3,800,000 troops (up from 1,700,000-2,000,000 in the late 1980s).

3. The Red Youth Guards made up of 14-16 year old school children. Although they receive two months of military training a year, they still need to be further trained for specialized tasks (such as air defense). They are expected to gradually take over local guard, defense and maintenance tasks as the Workers and Peasants Red Guards are transformed into part of the military and sent to the front. These youth are highly motivated and considered key to the DPRK's long-term ability to go on fighting and maintain popular resistance even under the most adverse conditions. The Red Youth Guards is estimated at 810,000-970,000 strong.

4. The People's Guard is comprised of the peace-time border guards and militarized civilian police, all integrated into units fiercely loyal to both Kim Il-Song and Kim Jong-Il. They serve as a Praetorian Guard, to go into action in the unlikely event that the Capital Defense Corps collapses and the enemy is marching on Pyongyang. The People's Guard is over 115,000 strong.

In addition, the KPA has over 1,240,000 soldiers, mainly young draftees, but also Guards in refresher courses or still in basic training. The KPA will hastily complete their training and then deploy them with the Workers and Peasants Red Guard units for deployment to the front-line. For the purpose of calculating the overall size of the KPA, it is not clear how many of these trainees are still off the books.

While the KPA were developing their capability to deliver a surprise attack on the South, they acquired large quantities of high-quality weapon systems from the USSR. Comparable weapons, though of lower quality, were also purchased from the PRC. The overall upgrading of the North Korean arsenal took place in two cycles.

The first cycle, in the late 1980s, was part of the strategic alliance consolidated between the USSR and the DPRK after Kim Il-Song's visit to Moscow in May 1984. This alliance revolutionized the KPA because it exposed its officers to the latest Soviet Art of War expertise. In return, the DPRK agreed to provide the USSR with access to several air bases and military sea ports, especially the ice-free Najin naval base. Moscow supplied MiG-23s, MiG-29s and Su-25s with up-to-date munitions and trained North Korean pilots on these and other sophisticated aircraft such as the Su-24. The USSR also provided the DPRK with SAM batteries (including SA-3b and SA-5), sophisticated radars, GCI, C3, and battle management systems. The KPA's Air Force was reorganized, with extensive Soviet help, around two air defense centers (near Sarlwon and Hamhung) that cover all of the DPRK and the ROK operational depth with SAMs. This deployment releases most of the jet fighters to offensive roles. The combat aircraft of the KPA Air Force are divided into 3 sectors: The Front, which is optimized for support of the deep offensive, and east and west, whose missions are to support the air defense and sustain offensive operations. (see fig.21)

The North Korean/Soviet close relationship was reaffirmed in January 1988 during the high level military discussions in Moscow between Marshal O Chin-U, Soviet Defense Minister D.T. Yazov and General I. Tret'yak, a former commander of the Far East TVD and then CiC of the Air Defense Forces. These strategic discussions were completed in April 1988 during Kim Il-Song's subsequent visit to Moscow and discussions with Mikhail Gorbachev. Several high level Soviet military delegations arrived in Pyongyang over the next few months to finalize details of the strategic cooperation and a naval task force led by the Commander of the Pacific Fleet visited Wonsan in May 1988. The Soviet Pacific Fleet and the KPA Fleet held annual joint naval exercises until December 1990. (see fig.22)

The collapse of the USSR had only positive effects on the DPRK because of Moscow's even further increased strategic interest in the Pacific rim. Indeed, North Korea embarked on the second cycle of major modernization of its Armed Forces with Russian/Soviet weapons in 1992-93. Gen.Col. Viktor Samsonov, the CIS Chief of the General Staff, and Gen. Choe Kwang, the DPRK Chief of the General Staff, signed a military cooperation agreement in Pyongyang on 3 March 1992 including provisions for the continuation of weapon supplies. (USSR/CIS weapon deliveries were briefly stopped in 1991 because of financial dis-

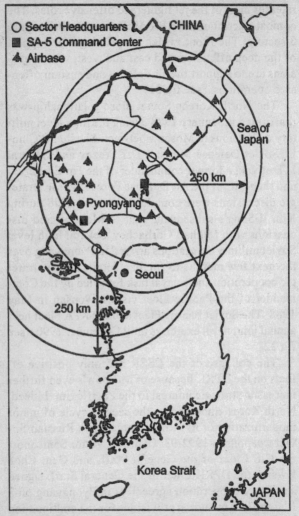

Fig 21 — The deployment of the KPA's air force and air defense system.

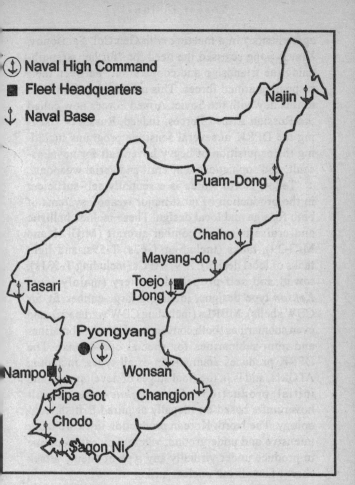

Fig 22 — The deployment of the KPA's navy.

agreements.) In a meeting with Gen.Col. Samsonov, Kim Il-Song stressed the need for "further strengthening the friendship and cooperation" between their respective armed forces. This relationship continues to this day with the Soviet Armed Forces now called the Russian Armed Forces. Indeed, Russia is assisting the DPRK in several sensitive programs including the acquisition of heavy hovercraft for naval assault, and sophisticated aircraft and aerial weapons.

Today, North Korea is essentially self-sufficient in the production of most major weapon systems of both foreign and local design. These include ballistic and cruise missiles, combat aircraft (MiG-21 and MiG-29), tanks (including T-62s, T-59s, and light tanks of local design), IFVs/APCs (including T-531s), towed and self-propelled artillery (mainly local *Koksan*-type designs, including large-caliber fit for CBW shells), MBRLs (including CBW warheads), and even submarines (both conventional attack submarines and mini-submarines for special operations). The DPRK produces ammunition of all types, including ATGMs, and is in the final stages of development and initial production of *Hwanghae*-type assault hovercrafts based on illegally acquired British technology. The North Korean production lines are labor intensive and underground, where they can continue to produce under virtually any type of enemy attack short of an all-out nuclear strike!

The KPA arsenal of early 1994 is not just impressive in size, but also demonstrates the extent of the build-up in the last year—that is since early 1993. At present, the KPA has some 3,800 tanks (including T-62s & T-72s), compared with 3,500 the year before. It has some 4,000 APCs/IFVs (some 300 of them

BMPs), including numerous new models of indigenous armored fighting vehicles introduced in 1993. The KPA artillery includes 3,600 towed guns/howitzers, 5,400 self-propelled guns/howitzers (including the latest 122mm, 152mm and even 175mm to 203mm SPGs), 2,400 MBRLs, over 80 SSMs, (up from 60 in 1993). The air defense has over 12,000 guns and 800 active SAMs (in 72 SA-2 batteries, 32 SA-3 batteries & 72 SA-5 batteries) and some 2,000 in storage. The air force has over 760-800 combat aircraft (including 46 MiG-23s, 24 MiG-29s, and 20 Su-25s), 170 armed helicopters (including 20 Mi-2s, 20 Mi-8s, 50 Mi-24s, and over 80 of the US-made Hughes 300 & 500), and 250 plus An-2s. Key to the navy are 24 attack submarines, at least 35 mini-submarines, and 194 amphibious craft (mainly semi-submersible high-speed craft). The DPRK also has well over 250 tons of chemical weapons—a stockpile that is increasing annually by 14 ton.

By the fall of 1992, at least 65% of the weapon systems needed by the KPA for the first phase of assault were within 100kms from the DMZ, all protected and sheltered. A recent defector from construction Unit 583 reported that the construction of "underground airstrips and underground naval bases" as well as other military facilities has been expanding markedly since 1991 on the basis of lessons learned from the US bombing of Iraq and in anticipation of an imminent war with the US. The DPRK also completed a new "wartime operations command post" some 100 meters below the Sosong District of Pyongyang, from where some 5,000 members of the elite will run the anticipated nuclear war with the West. This new super-bunker is connected through a myriad of tunnels, including the entire Pyongyang subway system, to a vast array of other underground military installations, all hardened to withstand nuclear strikes. Moreover, in the summer of 1992, the DPRK has already built-up a stockpile sufficient for 60 days of total war. The enlargement of these stockpiles continues with the near-term objective of 120 days worth of food and fuel.

16

THE KPA'S PREFERABLE WAR

Since the late 1980s and even more so in the early 1990s, the major modernization of the North Korean Armed Forces has centered on meeting the challenges of the modern battlefield while holding to the Forces' offensive doctrine. Confident of its military capabilities, Pyongyang adopted by the late 1980s the DPRK's strategic long-term planning still valid today. It envisions "reunifying" the Korean Peninsula "through armed force in 1995." According to 2nd.Lt. Kim Nam-Chun, who defected in September 1989, special intense training of KPA officer cadres has occurred to ready the KPA to "launch our attacks" by 1995.

A major aspect of this modernization and preparation program has been the greater North Koreanization of the theater, accounting for the reduction of reliance on possible reinforcements and resupplies from the USSR and the PRC. The development of the KPA's doctrine was described as "North

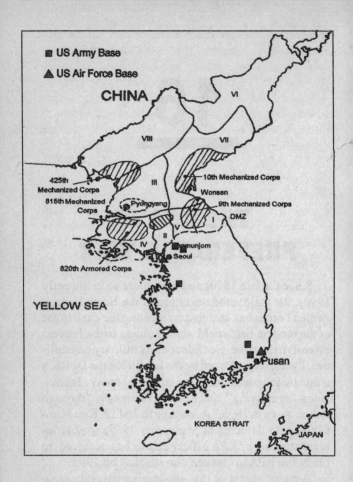

Fig 23 — The position of the main US military and air bases in South Korea relative to the KPA's deployment. Note that these facilities are clustered along the littoral avenue of advance, just south of Seoul and in the Pusan area.

Koreanized" version of Soviet art of war. Of the Soviet principles adopted, "the so-called in-depth maneuver is most important." Emphasis was put on massive use of highly mobile armoured thrusts with massive use of artillery and missile fire. Pyongyang sought to compentate for its loss of major components of military power by a reliance on the use of diversified special forces and weapons of mass destruction.

The integration of nuclear warfare into the KPA's art of war led to the further refinement of the entire North Korean doctrine. North Korean awareness of chemical warfare is reflected in all the DPRK tank and mechanized units, from army corps down to battalion, which have chemical warfare battalions as an integral component of the unit structure.

Pyongyang is convinced that the initial period of war is the most crucial. The DPRK intends to substitute surprise with the incitement of "revolutionary warfare" that is, the creation of chaos and terror, throughout South Korea. The DPRK has massive Special Forces optimized for deep operations aimed at preventing the South Korean and US forces from properly reacting to the last phases of Northern build-up, as well as effectively neutralizing their reaction to a North Korean offensive. These special operations will look like a grassroots struggle in South Korea, seeming to legitimize fraternal "assistance" from the North.

At this point, the main KPA forces will launch a lightening strike into the South in an effort to decide the war before massive reinforcements arrive from the US. The bulk of the DPRK Armed Forces are organized for such deep offensive operations. In order to have initial success it is imperative for the breakthrough offensive to be covered by a barrage of devastating fire suppression. The DPRK must also posses some weapons of mass destruction in order to balance the threat of US nuclear weapons.

The opening artillery and rocket barrage will be fired from a series of concealed forward positions. In the mid-1970s, the DPRK had already built more than 800 hardened artillery positions just north of the DMZ solely for firing this barrage. The KPA's weapons are constantly being upgraded. Their mechanized and armored units are saturated with all types of artillery, increasingly self-propelled. It was estimated in the early-1980s that with conventional munitions alone the initial artillery barrage and corresponding special operations would destroy some 20% of the forces in South Korea in the first 90 seconds of a conflict. Consequently, DPRK armored units will be able to reach Seoul in some 48 hours. The KPA's forward corps are located in a vast system of NBC-protected underground tunnels. Most of the SSMs in artillery pieces are also stored in hidden and protected shelters from which they can fire the opening salvo by surprise. (see fig.24)

Operating in two groups, the Tank Corps and the four Mechanized Corps will surge forward even before the initial artillery barrage is completed. In the west, the deep attack will be spearheaded by the 820th Armored Corps and the 815th Mechanized Corp, with the 425th Corps serving as the second eschelon. Their objective is the capture of Seoul, the destruction of the US forces in western ROK, and the occupation of the Korean coastline. Meanwhile, in the east, the 9th Mechanized Corps, followed by the 10th Mechanized Corps as a second echelon, will surge southwards along the eastern coast. Their primary objective is to

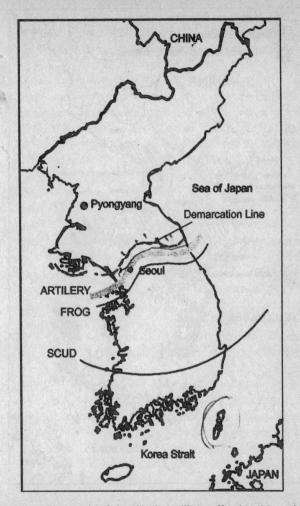

Fig 24 — The reach of the KPA's artillery offensive. Note that the DPRK's fully operational weapon systems (including the NKSCUD-C which maximum range is beyond this map) cover the entire peninsula, and are capable of striking at all the major military and urban centers of the ROK.

Fig 25 — The KPA's perception of the deep offensive on the Korean peninsula, phase 1: In the aftermath of the missile and artillery barrage, a wave of terrorism and spread all over South Korea. Meanwhile, the elite elements of the forward territorial Corps breach through the DMZ, overwhelming the defenders by their shere numbers. The first KPA units reach the outskirts of Seoul.

Fig 26 — The KPA's perception of the deep offensive on the Korean peninsula, phase 2: Once the DMZ area defenses are breached, the elite Armoured and Mechanized Corps surge forward and rapidly advance to encircle the peninsula. Meanwhile the main forces of the KPA expand their advance into central Korea. All these force movements exploit the ongoing escalation of the terrorist and special operations throughout the peninsula.

destroy the US forces in the Pusan area and link-up with the western force, thus completing the encirclement of the Korean peninsula. The large numbers of special forces and terrorists already inside South Korea are expected to sabotage and disrupt the entire rear in order to expedite the swift advance of the two KPA groups. (see fig.25)

The high-quality assests of the four Front Zone Corps will operate around the five Corps (Armored and Mechanized). The Front Zone Corps will first support the tank and mechanized Corps in breaking through the ROK's border fortifications. Then, once the five Corps have crossed into the ROK, the quality Corps will follow them into South Korea. They will be followed in quick succession by infantry corps. The infantry divisions comprising these corps are growing increasingly powerful and mobile, and acquiring artillery, air defense, anti-tanks weapons, and even armoured vehicles (APCs and tanks) as integral components. The main logic behind this build-up, which entails tremendous logistical efforts considering the huge number of infantry divisions—both standing and reserve—is to make them capable of advancing behind the armoured and mechanised spearheads as they encircle the peninsula. (see fig.26)

Furthermore, as the speed of advance of the high-quality forces increases in the strategic encirclement, they are less capable of destroying pockets of resistance. This task is now the responsibility of the fast moving infantry units. Indeed, in recent exercises infantry divisions are increasingly assigned heavy artillery units to meet the greater challenges of the modern battlefield. Furthermore, anti-tanks units, long associated with the high-quality assets, now cooperate with, and even are assigned to, the infantry divisions.

The DPRK's doctrine is now purely offensive based on surprise attack, high mobility, and shock tactics. Although Pyongyang hopes for a short victory, there is clear willingness to complete the mission even at the highest price and throughout a protracted war. Recent defectors reported that the KPA will try to neutralize the bulk of US/ROK forces near the DMZ, stop the arrival of US reinforcements, occupy (or isolate) Seoul, and bring the enemy to the point of demanding a cease fire and peace negotiations, all within seven days. Under present conditions, such a scenario has a good chance of success. It is highly likely that chemical weapons will be used in the offensive as needed. Of great importance is the contribution of the tens of thousands of special forces and terrorists expected to be activated in the rear of the ROK, thus opening a "second front" as destructive to US/ROK forces as the main front. (see fig.27 & 28)

Russian military analysts, who are among the best informed about the KPA, concur with this scenario. In early December 1993, their prediction was a North Korean victory within two weeks, mainly because sizable American reinforcements will not be able to reach Korea in time. The Russian experts emphasized that from the very beginning of any conflict, all airports and seaports in South Korea will be under such intense missile strikes and repeated raids that there will be no entry points into the South. Russian military analysts pointed out that, recently, the KPA has even further upgraded its aerial weaponry.

Washington is fully aware of the gravity of the military situation in Korea. Some American military

Fig 27 — The KPA's perception of the deep offensive on the Korean peninsula, phase 3: The Mechanized Corps complete the occupation of Seoul, as well as complete the encirclement of the peninsula. Meanwhile, the main KPA forces continue their steady advance, consolidating Pyongyang's hold over the territory.

Fig 28 — The KPA's perception of the deep offensive on the Korean peninsula, phase 4: Numerous KPA units, mainly regular infantry, close in on the Pusan area and the southern coast of the peninsula, completing the occupation of South Korea. The final suppression of the remnant pocket of resistance may take a long time, but new strategic realities have already been established.

experts fear that "the consequences of even a non-nuclear war there would be catastrophic."

In an analysis of options available to the US in the event of a North Korean offensive, even the best-case scenario is grim. In such a situation the US/ROK forces would retain control over the southern tip of the peninsula so that massive US reinforcements can be rushed in. Even then, the scenario envisions a "very high-intensity conflict" lasting, in the preferable option between 82 and 112 days or, in the more realistic case, well over four months and involving "roughly half [the US] major forces". In the process, the South Korean economy will have been almost completely destroyed. Some defense analysts consider this scenario very optimistic.

The worst-case scenario starts with the KPA swiftly completing the encirclement of the Korean coast before any sizable American reinforcements arrive. From here on, it is a political question of whether to mobilize the American nation and stage a major assault on the Korean peninsula. The minimal forces required for such an undertaking would exceed the current size of the US Armed Forces.

It should be emphasized that these scenarios, grim as they are, do not even begin to take into consideration such key factors as North Korean nuclear blackmail or the role of the PRC which still has a myriad of treaties in effect with the DPRK. A June 1993 textbook of the PLA High Command called *Can the Chinese Army Win the Next War?* identifies the US as the PRC's principal military adversary in the near future, and considers an intense war on the Korean peninsula as one of eight scenarios in which Beijing goes to war against the United States to defend its vital interests. In view of China's nuclear arsenal, any military conflict involving the PRC will be considered in Washington as a prelude to a world war.

Another key issue is the role of the DPRK's own nuclear weapons, especially as means of deterring or, at the least delaying, US intervention in the war. A threat from Pyongyang to use nuclear weapons, especially against Tokyo (Japan), or Vladivostok (Russia), is bound to attract attention in Washington. At the very least, deliberations in Washington on the appropriate reaction to the North Korean invasion and nuclear threat will take long enough for the KPA, by Pyongyang's own worst case calculations, to complete the encirclement of the Korean peninsula. At this point, the US will have already lost the possibility to implement its best-case scenario. According to a senior official of the South Korean Ministry of Defense Pyongyang is expected to use a nuclear threat. A senior official of the South Korean Ministry of Defense percieves that Pyongyang's strategy is "to initiate a surprise attack on the South, occupy some territory and negotiate for the termination of war, or to deny US reinforcement by threatening to use nuclear weapons."

North Korean officers who defected recently portray an even more chilling scenario for the possible use of the DPRK's few nuclear weapons in the event of a major crisis. They believe that Pyongyang will order a preemptive launch of nuclear strikes against a few select objectives in South Korea and Japan. "North Korea would attack US military bases in Japan and then launch air raids on Japan's major military bases," explains one defector. This scenario is similar to the PRC's early plans for a nuclear war, drawn by Marshal Lin Biao, in the late 1960s. The PRC identified three targets in Japan and one in South Korea whose destruction by nuclear weapons would cause immense numbers of American casualties. Beijing believed that "because America lacks nerve, any American President would choose to retreat in such a situation." Major worldwide pressure to avoid an escalation to a global nuclear war would further restrain the US. Under such circumstances, Beijing believed, "a weaker China could conquer a stronger America". Lin Biao, it should be remembered, was one of the main professional mentors of the DPRK's military elite.

Another potential North Korean ultimatum to the United States can come in the form of seaborne cruise missiles (such as the HY-2 SILKWORM), with biological warheads. Such missiles, which the DPRK is known to have, can be launched from the trawlers and cargo ships of the North Korean special forces. (The DPRK also produces launchers for these missiles for its FACs.) There should be no doubt that if such weapons are utilized, Washington will react with fury, obliterating the DPRK. The great danger, however, lies in the mere North Korean threat to use such weapons because it can again lead to the postponement of a reaction when the execution of the best-case scenario is still possible.

Meanwhile, since the Gulf War, where American military might and resolve were clearly demonstrated, Kim Jong-Il has been stressing the growing likelihood of a new Korean War as a result of what he called the New World Order.

Kim Jong-Il first used the New World Order to justify Pyongyang's growing militancy and his own involvement in military affairs, in the spring of 1991. He warned that the US was interested in "triggering a new war in Korea in particular" as part of a "vicious offensive against revolutionary countries," including the PRC. He urged a common strategy. "Crushing such a strategic attempt by the US imperialists is the most important and urgent task today for preventing a new war and safeguarding global peace."

In the face of the New World Order, the DPRK emphasized the unique loyalty and commitment of the military to the leadership and ideology. "Our people's powerful revolutionary Army rises up with formidable force to fulfill the orders of the party. There is no force on earth to match the invincible might of our People's Army which is firmly preparing itself to accomplish the revolutionary cause of *Juche* under the guidance of the party and the leader." Kim Jong-Il elaborated on the role of the KPA under challenging circumstances, "It is the great honor and pride of our party to have the People's Army that firmly defends the party and the leader and implements their orders even if it should go through fire and water."

It was in this context that General Choe Kwang, the Chief of the General Staff, outlined the military doctrine of the DPRK in late April 1991. He stressed that "our KPA has been firmly prepared not only politically and ideologically, but also technologically, becoming better strengthened and developed as an invincible revolutionary armed force equipped with intelligent strategy and tactics." Anticipating the need for mass mobilization, a major expansion of the training and replacement system was completed. In order to meet the challenges of the current battlefield, "the KPA is equipped with modern weapons, combat technology, and equipment." However, Choe Kwang emphasized, irrespective of the growing American threat, the primary objective of the KPA must remain the liberation of South Korea.

By mid 1991, Pyongyang found itself faced with two major challenges. There was the need to examine the ramifications of the American doctrine against the entire socialist world. And secondly, the succession process from Kim Il-Song to Kim Jong-Il. Both issues were addressed in a visit to PRC by Kim Il-Song (outlined below).

to Pyongyang...

PART III

TRANSFER OF POWER
IN PYONGYANG

By the spring of 1994, the DPRK had already reached a milestone in the transfer of powers from Kim Il-Song to his son Kim Jong-Il that will determine its future. The power position of Kim Jong-Il has risen markedly since late-July 1992 to the point of his emerging as the de-facto leader of North Korea. In the process, Pyongyang is committing itself to a profound ideological and strategic change.

Charting its future course, Pyongyang is actively preparing for a major military strike as a dramatic breakout from a global ideological deadlock and a collapsing economy. The timing of such an attack, if one occurs, will be coordinated with Syria and Iran in order to overwhelm the US and the West by forcing them to fight for the vital interest simultaneously in the Middle East and the Far East.

Meanwhile, North Korea is also opening up to economic relations with the West. In effect, the DPRK has adopted the Chinese model of relations with the West that separates economic development from strategic build-up. In February 1991, Chang Gon-Il, the Vice-President of the DPRK's Daesong Bank, alluded to Pyongyang's growing interest in import/export activities. He explained that *Juche* "is not producing and spending entirely by ourselves. We have potential and want to use it to its utmost."

Pyongyang, in effect, issues the West an ultimatum: either bail out the North Korean economy and finance the modernization of its military-dominated industrial basis or they will strike out against South Korea, shattering the stability of the entire Pacific rim.

These new developments are in essence the maturing of the North Korean grand strategy in the last few years. The celebrations of the 80th birthday of Kim Il-Song on 15 April 1992 were used to reinforce the posture of Kim Jong-Il as a worthy heir to the Great Leader, ensuring the continuation of their hold over North Korea.

17

CONSOLIDATION OF THE SUCCESSION PROCESS

The handing-over of the mantle from Kim Il-Song to Kim Jong-Il will establish the first "Communist Dynasty." The succession has been a lengthy and convoluted process with its roots back in April 1982 when Kim Il-Song went into "semi-retirement" after his 70th birthday and the death of Choe Hyon, his close friend and confidant for over 50 years. These events, more than anything else, brought age and frailty home to Kim Il-Song.

Thus, 1983 saw purges of the Pyongyang leadership by Kim Il-Song to remove possible opposition to a hereditary transfer of power. On 7 August 1984, Kim Jong-Il was officially identified as the successor.

Back in 1973, O Chin-U already made a secret announcement of this power transfer to the WPK leadership but nothing had been done to implement it. The main reason for that announcement was a sudden apprehension in Pyongyang about the effect of old age on Kim Il-Song.

Indeed, that year there was a sudden preoccupation at the highest levels in Pyongyang with the health of Kim Il-Song, especially his own realization of old age. In 1974, Pyongyang inaugurated the "Ponghwa Health Research Institute", a huge, sophisticated geriatric research facility with over 1,000 experts and countless staff, operating under the supervision of the "Committee for the Longevity of Kim Il-Song and His Son." The Institute monitors the health, diet and lifestyle of Kim Il-Song, and tests new medications on several North Korean citizens of similar build and age.

These institutes determined Kim Il-Song to be at a stage of semi-retirement. According to eye witnesses in the DPRK, Kim Il-Song is still "demonstrating his dynamic energy" in numerous travels and inspection tours all over the DPRK. However, the frequency of these trips continues to decline. In 1990, visitors to Pyongyang testified that he had "an energetic way that belied his old age....His back was straight and his voice seemed a little husky, but he looked sturdily healthy." Only the growth on the back of his neck seems bothersome.

Kim Il-Song enjoys the various resorts and villas he has in the countryside, all of them located 500 meters above sea level considered optimal for longevity. By 1990, his lifestyle was resembling that of the old Korean nobility, including the use of "happy groups" comprised of some 3,000 fair-skinned 20 year-old beauties, specially selected from all over the DPRK and educated for their challenging mission. The role of the "happy groups" is to contribute to the rejuvenation of Kim Il-Song through singing, dancing, and helping him bathe, washing and massaging his body. He maintains a special diet of natural and traditional Korean "health foods," with extremely old roots and other special fruits and spices collected from all over North Korea to ensure the purity of his diet.

A former member of Kim Il-Song's General Guard Bureau, the unit responsible for the security of both Kim Il-Song and Kim Jong-Il, recently provided first hand impressions of the several villas and places reserved for their activities. He served in Kim Il-Song's "Special House" in the Jamo Mountain, Pyongsong City, Pyongannam Do. In order to build this retreat, the DPRK leveled a whole mountain in the Jamo ridge to the precise altitude. In the place of the mountain, rolling hills and plateau were remade, a dense forest was planted, a lake was dug, and Kim Il-Song's favorite flowers were planted. The compound is so large that takes several hours to drive around the perimeter.

The organizing of hunting for Kim Il-Song is indicative of the extent to which Pyongyang goes to keep the Great Leader happy. A select population of specially adapted wild boar, deer and pheasants are grown in the forest. These animals are raised not to be afraid of people and cars. Consequently, Kim Il-Song can go "hunting" comfortably. He is driven in a specially modified Mercedes Benz sedan which virtually approaches the game. Then, Kim Il-Song fires from the window, and the Guards on hand bring the kill to the car. These animals are so used to people, the former guard recalled, that in certain cases, he and his friends had to kick the deer so that they moved closer to the Great Leader's car and were "hunted."

Kim Jong-Il is far more active. He was described in the mid 1980s as a "swaggering hothead." His guards describe him as "a playboy with a fussy temperament." Since the 1980s, he had frequent violent drinking bouts, some during state visits overseas. For example, he crashed a car while drunk in East Germany. In recent years, he was maintaining four mansions in the Pyongyang area, nine villas in the countryside, one near virtually every recreation spot for the elite as well as famous sites. Each house is fully staffed and stocked for the possibility he might drop in. He also has a collection of 30 expensive cars.

Kim Jong-Il has a central villa of his own, filled with the latest consumer goods and lavish items of comfort from the West. He increasingly uses the "happy groups," originally organized for his father, and is known for his very active and diverse sex life. In addition to members of these groups, he has had affairs with many of the DPRK's leading popular singers and actresses. For example, actress Hong Yong-Hui of the Revolutionary Opera is his "beloved concubine." He recently shot one actress for refusing to sleep with him.

Meanwhile, Pyongyang embarked on a transformation of the power structure from the older to the younger generation. Virtually, all of the newcomers are sons of Kim Il-Song's partisans and a few Soviet-Koreans (USSR-born Koreans brought to the North by the Soviet Armed Forces in 1945 to help build a Soviet-dominated regime in Pyongyang). Because the individuals involved received the best education North Korea and the Eastern Bloc had to offer, their rise to prominence also meant the introduction of more technocrats and professionals. The growing militancy of the DPRK has been the primary instrument of the younger generation to prove their revolutionary credentials and commitment to the legacy of Kim Il-Song.

This generation leap in Pyongyang provides unique circumstances for the reexamination of the *Juche* doctrine, now also called Kimilsongism. Ultimately changes proved to be primarily an adaptation of existing policy. Pyongyang retains its commitment to confrontation with the West.

A major development in Pyongyang's world view resulted from Kim Il-Song's visit to the PRC in October 1991. The visit was originally intended to ensure Beijing's support for Kim Il-Song's long-term hold over power. The extension of the visit from four days to 10 days just prior to Kim Il-Song's departure suggested a decision to discuss major issues of the highest importance for both countries. Pyongyang pointed out that "Great Leader Comrade Kim Il-Song's visit to the PRC will be an epoch-making event with historic significance for strengthening the traditional DPRK-China friendship and for the victory of the socialist cause."

The significant decisions were reached in the conclusion of the discussions. The Chinese explained that their decision to provide the DPRK with comprehensive assistance, "was made as part of its [PRC's] reformulation strategy to make North Korea and other socialist countries into strategic bases for anti-US activities in the wake of the Soviet situation." However, Beijing admitted that it is unable to finance the rejuvenation of the militant socialist bloc, and unwilling to risk the loss of its ties with the West. Instead, the Chinese pressured Kim Il-Song to adopt the Chinese approach, explaining that better economic relations with the West will improve economic posture, permit massive hi-tech imports, and relieve internal opposi-

Yossef Bodansky

tion pressures. Getting rich, the Chinese insisted, does not constitute giving up one's revolutionary anti-imperialist credentials. Moreover, the hi-technology imported in the process improves military capabilities while reducing the hostility and vigilance of the enemy. After lengthy deliberations, Pyongyang finally accepted this world view in the summer of 1992.

North Korea is experiencing an acute shortage of fuel to the point of near paralysis. Both Japan and Russia believed that Kim Il-Song was on the verge of collapse because of the severity of the DPRK's economic problems. But Pyongyang started storing wartime fuel reserves and by late 1992, they had built a substantial stockpile.

Sharing an urgent need for a dramatic breakout from the "New World Order," North Korea signed a major agreement with Iran in March 1991, providing the oil required by the DPRK, especially high-quality jet fuel, in return for strategic weapons and technologies.

Meanwhile, the shortage of fuel had created a shortage of energy. Pyongyang began using a "staggered-production system," to save energy. It is also building alternate-energy power stations including those using thermal and nuclear energy.

The current crisis has resulted in an apparent reduction in militarization. These changes are officially attributed to Kim Jong-Il's guidance by the "decision": "We must hold on firmly to the central task of the light industry revolution and bring about a new turnaround in the production of consumer goods for the people." This campaign is identified as the development of the "August 3 Movement" named after the visit by Kim Jong-Il to a factory on 3 August 1984 where he issued directives to improve productivity and diversify production.

In reality, this campaign serves as a cover and an excuse for the modernization of military-related industries. Indeed, a closer examination of the "consumer goods" on Pyongyang's list points to the commitment to development of industries with dual-use.

A critical component of Kim Jong-Il's modernization effort is access to Western hi-tech. Toward this end, in the fall of 1992, the DPRK worked out a program to induce $100m worth of foreign investment from the West that will also bring about a fundamental modernization of hi-tech capabilities, especially the production of computers and semi-conductor technology. The North Koreans negotiated 18 projects, involving annual production of 20,000 32-bit personal computers and 20 million sophisticated semi-conductors including the silicon monocrystal wafers, as well as diversified dual-use electronic consumer goods. The completion of these projects will result in the introduction of a new generation of production technologies, computer-controlled machine tools, and electricity-generating equipment. International companies are paid well to violate COCOM regulations by bringing illegal hi-tech into North Korea. Indeed, in late 1993, the DPRK already acquired large numbers of computer components for 486-type microprocessors, thus accelerating their own entry into computer production.

Japan was to be the primary source of hi-tech and financial assistance for North Korea. Pyongyang believes that it can pressure Tokyo into saving the North Korean economy and financing the modernization effort. In late-July 1992, Pyongyang reiterated that Japan must "repent her past wrongs" by providing massive economic assistance and financial compensation. However, because of demands from Japan, discussions between the two countries are deadlocked with no date set for resumption. Pyongyang did not react to Tokyo's offer to meet in Beijing in late-July.

The DPRK's economic situation continues to deteriorate, and its dependence on the PRC and Iran grows. Fearing economic collapse, Pyongyang finally accepted Beijing's urging to adopt a comparable strategic and political line of economic relations with the West. However, this compromise would not alter the commitment to the confrontational grand strategy. Moreover, Pyongyang is not convinced that these changes in economic foreign policy can prevent the threat of imminent collapse. Thus, from their perspective, the subjugation of South Korea seems like the only way to ensure the survival of the current regime in Pyongyang. Coupled with urgings from Tehran to join the struggle against the US, strengthened by the offer of further lucrative oil deals, Pyongyang is tilting more and more toward a drastic solution.

Indeed, in late-July 1992, North Korea began warning of a major deterioration in inter-Korean relations. Pyongyang warned that South Korea has recently "accelerated its arms build-up behind the scenes" because Seoul is "not interested in peaceful reunification." South Korea can carry out this dangerous maneuver because of the enduring US "nuclear blackmail policy intended to maintain the state of confrontation and tension on the Korean peninsula." Pyongyang accuses Seoul of "inciting distrust and confrontation between the North and the South," and of adopting aggressive policies "making it impossible to smoothly discuss the basic issues." Thus, Pyongyang warns that the continuation of this situation can lead to unforeseen complications, namely, the eruption of fighting.

In August 1992, North Korea also embarked on a high-level coordination of policies and strategies with Syria and Iran, in anticipation of a forthcoming crisis and possibly even a war. The DPRK and Iran also agreed on the further expansion of several joint projects including additional oil-for-weapons technology deals.

18

PREPARING FOR A NEW LEADER AND WAR

Meanwhile, as of late-July 1992, when these developments were taking place, Pyongyang embarked on the final phase of transferring power from Kim Il-Song to Kim-Jong Il. North Korea's future challenges, goals and doctrine have been clearly stated in the course of this process.

The campaign started with an emphasis on the urgency of defending socialism in a hostile world environment, made all the more difficult because of the collapse of so many communist countries. Compromise is inconceivable because "the goal is to safeguard, defend, and advance socialism." Pyongyang points to the complexity of the challenges presented by the West. "In recent years the imperialists have threatened socialist countries with nuclear weapons and tempted them with dollars. They have also [inserted corruption] into socialist countries."

The DPRK remains committed to "a resolute

struggle against imperialism." Pyongyang believes that the worsening world situation increases the likelihood of an offensive. "Countering the enemies with a revolutionary offensive when their counter-revolutionary offensive intensifies is exactly our party's traditional struggle method."

Pyongyang holds Kim Jong-Il to be the key to the future of the DPRK and its military might. "A brighter prospect lies in the road ahead for our People's Army, because it upholds the Dear Leader, Comrade Kim Jong-Il, as the supreme commander of the Korean People's Army. The Dear Leader, Comrade Kim Jong-Il, is firmly building our revolutionary armed forces into an invincible one. He has built the People's Army into invincible militant ranks that can defeat any aggression."

Only Kim Jong-Il, as the chosen son of Kim Il-Song is capable of being the true heir to the Leader. "Because of this, the unity and cohesion of the leader, the party, and the masses are inherited generation after generation and are solidified as firm as a rock. ... Nothing can shake our people's faith to strengthen the wholehearted unity of the leader, the party, and the masses, to brilliantly inherit and develop the *Juche* revolutionary tradition with that might, and to complete the revolution to the end." It is noteworthy that the most important original goal remaining unresolved is the unification of the Korean peninsula.

Kim Jong-Il was originally identified only as "member of the Presidium of the Political Bureau of the Central Committee of the Workers Party of Korea and Secretary of the Party Central Committee." He was now identified as "the military genius and the Supreme Commander of the Korean People's Army."

(Kim Jong-Il was awarded the rank of Marshal of the DPRK, along with 8 other senior officers, and identified as supreme commander of the KPA on 20 April 1992, after Kim Il-Song's 80th birthday, but there was no indication of the title's being anything more than part of the personality cult.)

In early-August 1992, the unprecedented importance of Kim Jong-Il was clarified in a statement emphasizing that the DPRK is entering "a new revolutionary upsurge" made possible by the able leadership of the Dear Leader. Pyongyang then provided the first clear indication of Kim Jong-Il's new prominence: "It is the firm will of the entire party to faithfully struggle under the leadership of the Dear Leader, Comrade Kim Jong-Il, holding the Great Leader Comrade Kim Il-Song in high esteem."

Two days later, a new phase in the development of the traditional *Juche* was introduced under the title of the New Kimjongilism. Both Radio Pyongyang and Central TV carried a prime time report on a letter sent by the widow of a senior official vowing to raise her children to serve the revolution. The significance in this "letter" is that she referred to the DPRK as "the fatherland of Kimjongilism." Since then, there has been a growing frequency of the use of Kimjongilism in the North Korean media along with other signs of "accelerating the last-stage of the power succession by putting the idolization of Kim Jong-Il onto the same level as that of Kim Il-Song."

19

THE WAR THAT ALMOST WAS

Pyongyang's anticipation of war in the fall of 1992 caused a slow down in the succession process. There are strong indications that Kim Il-Song was determined to formally be the Supreme Leader and personally lead the major attempt to unify the Korean peninsula by force and take on the US. Indeed, steps were immediately taken to shield Kim Jong-Il and contain his rise to power. Most notably, Kim Jong-Il was supposed to lead the DPRK's delegation to the Non-Aligned Summit in Jakarta in early September 1992. The Summit was to serve as his formal introduction as the leader of North Korea and several meetings were being arranged for him with attending leaders. However, he was replaced at the last minute.

A few days later, a high level Iranian delegation led by President Hashemi-Rafsanjani visited Pyongyang to discuss the final coordination of their strategic surge. While Pyongyang remained, at that time, committed to going to war on the eve of the US elections and implementing the joint grand design, some of the Iranians came back with the impression that self-confidence was lacking at the highest levels of the DPRK's leadership. The Iranians' reading of Pyongyang was that Kim Il-Song was too old to lead, and nobody, including Kim Il-Song himself, really trusted Kim Jong-Il to be able to lead the country through a crisis that amounted to a world war. Indeed, the DPRK had cold feet at the last minute.

The main reason for the sense of insecurity and lack of self-confidence in Pyongyang seems to have been the reluctance of the members of the high commands of the armed forces to get involved in the anticipated military adventures. The doubts in, and reluctance of, a number of senior officers reached such a level that the question of their loyalty to Kim Il-Song and Kim Jong-Il was raised. In September 1992, 18 officers, about 10 of them generals, began contemplating the advisability and possibility of a coup attempt in order to effect modernization and liberalization in the DPRK. All of them were Soviet educated and influenced by *Perestroika*. The plot was immediately betrayed to the security police by a participant and all 18 were seized and promptly executed. According to a recent defector, a KPA junior officer who claims to have first hand knowledge of the coup, the plotting officers were echoing widespread sentiments in the Armed Forces. As part of the coup plans, military units stationed near Pyongyang would storm the presidential palace and other key government buildings and kill both Kim Il-Song and Kim Jong-Il.

There is no evidence that the implicated senior officers ever reached a point of discussing their plans

with others. Thus, the plans discussed by the defector
may be part of other coup designs or just the expression of hostile sentiments. Since the consolidation of
Kim Jong-Il's power relies on the support of the military, it was imperative for Pyongyang to reassert its
firm hold over the high command before any crisis
was contemplated. With both Moscow and Beijing
already cool to the idea of a World War instigated by
Iran and its allies on the eve of the US elections, the
DPRK had an excuse to renege on its commitment to
take part. Indeed, there was no eruption in the fall of
1992.

20

ACCELERATION OF THE SUCCESSION PROCESS

Meanwhile, the medical condition of Kim Il-Song continued to deteriorate during the summer. The difficulties he had chewing and swallowing rice grew to the point that he frequently needed napkins to wipe his face. He was becoming tired more easily to the point that Kim Jong-Il ordered that meetings be limited to less than an hour at a time. Moreover, Kim Il-Song was in increasing pain because the tumor on his neck was growing again, pressuring some of his nerves. Kim Il-Song's visible short temper and, at times, mild agitation, were attributed to the pain in the neck.

These visible signs, as well as a host of internal problems, resulted in an overall worsening of Kim Il-Song's medical condition. In October 1992, Kim Jong-Il appealed to Beijing to send a team of senior medical experts led by one of Beijing's leading Party physicians to treat his father. According to Japanese sources, the Chinese doctors concluded that the condition of Kim Il-Song was worse than anticipated and he was hospitalized. There were signs of nervous disorder problems. The Chinese doctors ordered that Kim Il-Song's lifestyle be relaxed, that he be provided only with good news, engage only in enjoyable activities, and that he be committed to bed early and for long hours. Kim Jong-Il immediately ordered that these recommendations be implemented.

Ultimately, the primary conclusion Pyongyang drew from the visit of the Chinese medical experts was that the transfer of power to Kim Jong-Il must be expedited immediately.

In late November 1992, the succession issue was revived and presented as a major indication of the success of the Party. "Our party has strengthened and developed into a powerful ruling party under socialism. The key to all these successes lies in that it has properly solved the question of inheriting the leadership."

Despite Pyongyang's reluctance to go to war in the fall of 1992, the DPRK has not given up on implementing the joint grand design with the PRC, Iran, and Syria, once conditions are ripe. In late November 1992, Pyongyang revived the warnings about the growing threat of war and the emphasis that resolute steps were imperative for the country's survival. "The imperialists' moves to stifle the people's independence are getting more vicious. This requires that the anti-imperialist struggle be waged vigorously. ... In order to realize the people's independence, it is imperative first of all for all the anti-imperialist independent forces to pull their strength in a common front. Only then will their strength be increased beyond measure and successfully smash the imperialists." There was a major deviation from the past in that this time Pyongyang was endorsing a diverse alliance against the US. In a clear endorsement of the alliance with Iran and its Islamic Bloc, Pyongyang emphasized that "the anti-imperialist independent forces must smash the imperialists' moves for division and alienation and firmly unite under the banner of anti-imperialist independence, transcending the differences in ideology and social system, nation and religious belief."

Another "first" was the mention that the anti-imperialist struggle would be waged under the leadership of Kim Jong-Il. In early December, special attention was paid to strengthening and further legitimizing the position of Kim Jong-Il as the KPA's supreme commander. There was a clear and visible need for the military elite to reiterate and emphasize their loyalty to Kim Jong-Il. "The infinite loyalty of the KPA to the people and the leader [Kim Il-Song] ... is now reaching the highest level in holding Comrade Kim Jong-Il in high esteem as its supreme commander."

In an early December conference of the senior officers overseeing the League of Socialist Working Youth of Korea [LSWYK] within the ranks of the KPA, Minister of Defense Marshal O Chin-U, the closest confidant of Kim Il-Song, further encouraged new vows of loyalty, stressing that LSWYK leaders "should educate all youth soldiers to live and struggle with the soldier's spirit of unhesitatingly jumping into fire and water according to the supreme commander's order."

While the North Korean economy continued to collapse in late 1992, Kim Jong-Il was increasingly featured as the leader of innovation and progress. He was cited as an authority on the importance of self-sufficiency and a self-reliant economy. He revived calls for power conservation and for finding new methods for power production, primarily coal and thermal plants. There was a major mobilization of soldiers to build power plants and other "power generation facilities" in a series of crash programs.

In civilian, consumer goods factories, production fell to 30% of capacity due to acute shortages in energy, but in a sharp contrast, military production continued around the clock. This disparity in production rates would further increase during the first half of 1993.

According to Ko Chong-Son, a recent defector, there were unprecedented food shortages all over the country as of the fall of 1992. The basic individual food ration (10% rice, 90% corn) was reduced in the fall of 1992 from 700 grams a day to 550 grams a day. There have been up to three month delays in the delivery of corn, compelling people to eat wild grass. The collapse of the food supply system sunk to the point that even army personnel, the best fed in the country, suffered malnutrition at times. Meat is available once or twice a year, usually on holidays associated with Kim Il-Song and Kim Jong-Il. The price, however, of 1kg of meat is equivalent to a month's salary.

The shortages of food are so acute that "Let's Eat Two Meals a Day, not Three!" is a frequently seen billboard all over the rural parts of the DPRK. Recent travelers reported acute shortages of most basic foods and goods. Still, contrary to reports of a growing number of food riots all over the country, there is no real vocal opposition due to constant fear of secret police. All together, there were only five or six riots of note in 1991-1992 and all were crushed swiftly and ruthlessly. There has not been any increase in public activism recently despite the visible marked deterioration in living conditions. The primary reason for this passivity is increased repression. Rapidly growing numbers of soldiers and secret police are seen all over North Korea.

The economic situation in the DPRK deteriorated to the point of the near extortion of rich Japanese-Korean tourists who are encouraged to visit their relatives in the North. These tourists are told to bring food, clothes, and black-market goods to their relatives. North Korean luxury liners meanwhile also deliver used cars and trucks between Asian markets to generate revenues. Some of these cars were stolen in Hong Kong and smuggled to the PRC where they are loaded on North Korean ships for transfer to lucrative markets in Asia. Furthermore, a DPRK diplomat was caught in Beijing in late August 1993 selling US$ in the black market for local currency in order to stretch the sharply shrunken budget of the embassy.

A major leap forward in the consolidation of Kim Jong-Il as the DPRK's leader took place on 10 December 1992, during the 20th plenary meeting of the 6th Central Committee of the Workers Party of Korea [WPK]. The meeting was a rare one-day purge. It brought to the top several people close and to Kim Jong-Il, who are also economic experts. Reflecting the importance of these personnel changes, Kim Il-Song ordered the purges and the new appointments to key government positions, thus legitimizing Kim Jong-Il's younger loyalists.

Most important was the re-nomination of Kang Song-San, already the President of the DPRK, as the new Premier. Kang Song-San is the most important second generation leader in the DPRK's hierarchy and his identification with Kim Jong-Il will enhance his position.

Other key appointments in the Pyongyang government included: Kim Hwan who was appointed Vice-Premier and Minister of Chemical Industry. He is an outstanding hi-tech expert. Yi Song-Tae was appointed Chairman of the External Economic Committee. Kim Tal-Hyon, was "dismissed" as Chairman of the External Economic Committee and nominated Vice-Premier of the Administration Council and Chairman of the State Planning Committee. The son of Kim Il-Song's cousin, he is trusted with such sensitive issues as handling hard currency. Kim Yong-Sun was nominated the Director of the WPK's International Department where he is expected to accelerate his effort to establish economic and political relations with the US and Japan.

Three key ministerial nominations were Kang Song-San, Kim Tal-Hyon, and Kim Yong-Sun who are described as "close confidants to Kim Jong-Il." They are his economic team and will oversee his economic reform policy. In addition, most of the ministers of industry and other economic activities, as well as many senior legal officials, were "dismissed" by Kim Il-Song. The December 10 reshuffle should be seen as a drastic measure to expedite economic reforms.

Other promotions within the WPK's structure indicate additional future changes at and near the top: Kim Kuk-Tae, the Director of Cadre Affairs will promote and demote people for Kim Jong-Il. Kim Ki-

Nam, the Director of the Propaganda and Agitation Committee of the WPK's Central Committee, will build the image of the Dear Leader at the helm. They are also close confidants of Kim Jong-Il, himself currently WPK Secretary in charge of Organization, and enjoy his trust. They worked together for several years. Their support and cooperation will be crucial in the inevitable effort by Kim Jong-Il to purge and mold the DPRK's leadership. In addition, a Kim Il-Song devotee, Yi Pong-Kil, was nominated Chairman of the Central Control Committee of the WPK, ensuring that the Great Leader's interest is not sacrificed in the transition period.

However, in a sharp contrast, Kim Il-Song did not relinquish the firm hold of his fierce loyalists over the military. Marshal O Chin-U remains in the military. It is highly important that proven old hands remain in leadership positions during any war. O Chin-U's remaining in position also expresses Kim Il-Song's determination to retain actual leadership for the war of unification.

The DPRK's Military elite remains a combination of Kim Il-Song's own loyalists, with a growing number of Kim Jong-Il's next generation people. Back in February 1988, Choe Kwang, a Kim Il-Song devotee, was promoted to Chief of the General Staff. Since then, while in office, Choe Kwang proved himself "a key supporter of Kim Jong-Il" in several key military and political forums. Choe Kwang's predecessor as Chief of General Staff, O Kuk-Yol, "regarded as Kim Jong-Il's right hand man," is being educated and groomed for a higher position, probably as the replacement for O Chin-U once Kim Jong-Il assumes power formally. O Kuk-Yol is a military reformer and advocate of hi-tech weaponry. His hand in the rising profile of the DPRK's defense industries is increasingly apparent.

In early-December, a high-level North Korean delegation visited Iran and signed "a memorandum of understanding" on long-term joint projects ranging from weapons development to establishing a maintenance system for Iran's growing arsenal of East bloc weapons. Iranian officials had doubts about the agreement due to North Korea's succession problem, "North Korea is basically an unstable state and the political situation there might deteriorate to unknown dimensions after the death of its leader Kim Il-Song, who is 82 years old." Since 1980, Iran has been one of the closest allies of the DPRK and several Iranian officials spent very long periods there, getting unique insight into the innermost power corridors of Pyongyang. Their apprehension is therefore significant.

In a statement discussing North Koreas military strength in late December 1992, Kim Jong-Il's position was further consolidated. Pyongyang stressed the importance of the military's loyalty to Kim Jong-Il. "In upholding the Supreme Commander, our people's army is preparing itself in military technique so as to defeat any formidable enemy." This statement, though propagandistic, nevertheless hinted anew the possibility of a confrontation with the US. It also repeatedly identified Kim Jong-Il without mentioning Kim Il-Song at all. For example, "The KPA is firmly resolved to tenaciously upholding Comrade Kim Jong-Il, its supreme commander."

In one of these statements, dealing with the unique influence of Kim Jong-Il's military knowledge, the title and position of Kim Jong-Il were elevated further. He was now referred to as "the Great Leader and the Great Commander" and the KPA was referred to as the "revolutionary Army that upholds the dear Comrade Kim Jong-Il as the Great Leader of our party and revolution and as the supreme commander of our revolutionary Armed Forces." (Throughout most of the article, Kim Jong-Il was referred to as the Dear Leader, his usual title.) The personality cult superlatives describing Kim Jong-Il's military skills and knowledge reached unprecedented heights. For example, "The Dear Leader Comrade Kim Jong-Il is truly the great, brilliant general who has clairvoyant, extraordinary military knowledge, strategy, unrivaled courage, and outstanding tactics. The ultimate victory of our revolutionary cause rests with the fact that we uphold Comrade Kim Jong-Il, the respected and beloved supreme commander of our revolutionary armed forces, as the Republic's Marshal." This statement, with a very few changes, was repeated more than a dozen times in one article alone.

Further indication of the succession was expressed by the Chief of the General Staff, Choe Kwang, in a speech to senior officials of the military and defense establishment. He repeatedly referred to Kim Jong-Il as "a unique military strategist" and "supreme commander of the KPA. Choe Kwang specifically attributed Kim Jong-Il's rise to a decision of Kim Il-Song, thus sanctifying the move, and went on to define Kim Jong-Il's modernization effort as a milestone in the development of the KPA in anticipation of the challenges ahead. "The Great Leader Comrade Kim Il-Song taught us: Our People's Army guided by supreme commander Kim Jong-Il is sure to win every battle with any strong enemy. ... By upholding dear Comrade Kim Jong-Il, the great sagacious commander, as its supreme commander, our People's Army further strengthened its military and technological might as an unrivaled power capable of smashing any strong imperialist army in this world." As Choe Kwang was ending his speech, the audience rose to their feet shouting "Long Live Comrade Kim Jong-Il!"

21

WARNING SIGNS AND A NEW CRISIS

For years, the North Korean media have been circulating endless personality cult reports about Kim Il-Song's advice to, and interest in, virtually any conceivable project in the country. Nevertheless, Kim Il-Song's sudden interest in one such project might be of significance if only because of the media's preoccupation with the issue.

Between 29 December 1992 and mid January 1993, there was daily coverage of Kim Il-Song's preoccupation with the reconstruction of the Tomb of King Tongmyong, including a few on-site visits to give the workers guidance. (Kim Il-Song had last visited the tomb in April 1989.) Quite possibly he is coming to grips with his own mortality. Japanese diplomats who frequent Pyongyang claim the North Korean media's preoccupation with Kim Il-Song and the Tomb fueled rumours about a deterioration in Kim Il-Song's health, all the way to speculation about his imminent death.

Added to this is the fact that Kim Il-Song's new year's greetings speech, usually broadcast live just after midnight, was pre-recorded this year. The address itself was a repetition of old slogans and ideological motives. However, the official commentary and highlights of Kim Il-Song's address, carried by all media organs (radio, TV, papers, etc.) added two intriguing commentaries. "We must open a new phase in the struggle for national unification this year," Pyongyang interpreted, adding that "our socialist cause will be ever-victorious and our victory in this year's struggle is certain." The time factor, that is the imminence of the struggle, had not been mentioned by Kim Il-Song at all.

The second media commentary on Kim Il-Song's address was even more telling. "Our people are firmly convinced that our socialism will be ever-victorious as long as the Dear Leader Comrade Kim Jong-Il, with an experienced and tested art of leadership, wisely guide the overall affairs of our party, state and Army." In his speech, Kim Il-Song did not even allude to Kim Jong-Il, let alone mention him by name! Thus, Pyongyang's addition to the address reflects the new reality in the DPRK.

In the spring of 1993, the medical condition of Kim Il-Song, North Korea's Great Leader, worsened to the point that the leadership in Pyongyang began actively preparing for Kim Il-Song's imminent death.

The Chinese medical team was rushed back to Pyongyang in late January or early February in order to examine and treat Kim Il-Song. Reportedly, their conclusion was that very little could be done. Indeed, in early February 1993 Pyongyang was awash with rumors about the serious illness and near death condition of Kim Il-Song to the point that a Spanish official then visiting Pyongyang was rushed to a meeting with Kim Il-Song only in order to have a foreigner confirm that the Great Leader was still alive.

Indeed, a most telling indication of Kim Il-Song's imminent death was the canceled purchase of $100 million worth of gifts for his birthday, indicating that the Great Leader would probably not be alive on his next birthday.

This development was coming at the same time as the crisis over North Korea's nuclear weapons. The development of nuclear weapons had always been a high priority project of Kim Jong-Il. He was behind both North Korea's acceptance of IAEA inspections, in order to gain international legitimacy and encourage the flow of high technology to the North, and subsequently its sudden withdrawal from the Non-Proliferation Treaty when the IAEA inspectors were getting too close to discovering the nuclear program.

However, Kim Jong-Il exploited the international condemnation for North Korea's move and the annual joint military exercises of the US and South Korea called Team Spirit 93 in order to create a major regional crisis. He would use the national emergency as an instrument to consolidate his total control over the military. Pyongyang clearly identified Kim Jong-Il as being responsible for the March 9 declaration of the "Semi-War State," which, had it escalated further, would have led to a "Sacred War for Reunification."

Moreover, Kim Jong-Il issued the call for the "voluntary" mobilization of several millions of reservists as well as some 1.5 million additional people regularly outside the mobilization mechanism. Kim Jong-Il ordered the stand down of the war readiness after a few tense days but throughout this crisis, he had clearly demonstrated complete control over North Korea's national defense, thus, in effect, putting himself effectively in the position of the national leader.

It is note worthy that the current crisis occurred even before Kim Jong-Il had been able to complete the positioning of his loyalists in all the power positions. Kim Jong-Il's increased control over the military has been achieved and clearly demonstrated through the replacement of some 664 generals since April 1992. All of the promoted officers are younger technocrats, loyal to Kim Jong-Il. However, Kim Jong-Il had to leave the Minister of Defense O Chin-U (83) and the Chief of the General Staff Choe Kwang (76), both fiercely loyal to Kim Il-Song, in their very powerful, yet isolated, positions at the top.

Thus, the mere fact that Kim Jong-Il found it necessary to embark on a national crisis almost leading to a war with the US and South Korea even before he had his own loyalists at the helm, strongly urged Pyongyang to complete the transfer of power from Kim Il-Song to Kim Jong-Il.

22

THE BEGINNING OF THE END OF THE SUCCESSION PROCESS

Between 8 and 9 April 1993, after the "Semi-War State" crisis, the DPRK passed yet another major milestone in the transfer of power from Kim Il-Song to his son Kim Jong-Il.

On April 8, Kim Jong-Il was elected Chairman of the National Defense Committee, the supreme defense body of the DPRK. This position was one of the crucial power posts held by Kim Il-Song. The official announcement emphasized that the national command powers were now in the hands of Kim Jong-Il. "Comrade Kim Jong-Il, Supreme Commander of the Korean People's Army, was elected chairman of the National Defense Commission," Pyongyang announced. In itself, the current nomination of Kim Jong-Il was a logical development for he had been appointed Supreme Commander of the Korean People's Army in

December 1991 and awarded the rank of Marshal in April 1992. As Chairman of the National Defense Committee, Kim Jong-Il is in effect the DPRK's Commander in Chief.

The sudden nomination of Kim Jong-Il was an integral part of the expedited final transfer of power from Kim Il-Song. The formal nomination of Kim Jong-Il was conducted in a suddenly assembled fifth session of the Ninth Supreme People's Assembly. There is no evidence that Kim Il-Song took part in the session.

In the course of the "Semi-War State" crisis, Kim Jong-Il reiterated and demonstrated his commitment to the North Korean nuclear program, and the unification of Korea by force, his father's sacred mission. Consequently, he gained the strong support of the upper echelons of the Armed Forces, the element most loyal to Kim Il-Song.

There were other signs that Kim Il-Song is about to die. On April 12, the North Korean authorities suddenly canceled all the visas and permits for foreign journalists to cover Kim Il-Song's birthday (April 15). Many of these were staunch loyalists of the regime repeatedly invited by Pyongyang for such occasions. Even Chinese guests were denied permits despite protestations of the PRC embassy.

On April 15, Kim Il-Song showed up to his 81st birthday banquet in Pyongyang. Several dignitaries from North Korea's closest allies, such as the PRC, Iran, Syria, Pakistan, and Cambodia, were present at the banquet. In his speech, Kim Il-Song stressed points now clearly associated with the primary policies pursued by Kim Jong-Il, thus further sanctifying the transfer of authority. Kim Il-Song referred to the IAEA inspection regimes as violations of the DPRK's sovereignty and dared the US to do something about the North Korean defiance. "Our republic, which regards independence as its lifeblood, will never tolerate its sovereignty being violated," he stated. "The imperialists and reactionaries are trying to apply 'sanction' against us in order to isolate and crush our republic, on the excuse of a nuclear problem which does not actually exist. ... But no threat or power politics will have any effect on us," Kim Il-Song concluded.

The DPRK's sacred Army Day, April 25, passed with virtually no celebrations or public events. Neither Kim Il-Song nor Kim Jong-Il appeared in public, a very perplexing omission considering the recent elevation of Kim Jong-Il to the key military position of chairman of the National Defense Commission.

Since late April 1993, a series of internal military moves began in the DPRK that strongly suggested an imminent crisis. First, Kim Jong-Il ordered the transfer of 3 divisions with over 1,700 armored vehicles away from the zone between Pyongyang and the DMZ to the Chinese border. This was the largest troop movement since the Korean War. The reason for the re deployment was a fear that these army units might be loyal to the old guard military high command and thus be used to deny Kim Jong-Il the rise to power.

Meanwhile, starting in early April, the Sunan airport, north of Pyongyang closed for repairs. Virtually all international flights were diverted to Wonsan. However, the Sunan airport is in good shape and key political/official flights, including those of Prince Norodom Sihanouk in and out of Cambodia, continue to use Sunan.

The reason for the closing down of Sunan became

apparent in late April. Large units of the fiercely loyal Special Forces were deployed to the Sunan area. The size and character of the units suggest either active preparations for a military coup, or the preemptive positioning against the possibility of one. The build-up of forces in Sunan continued to grow by May 1993.

In mid May, Chinese officials added fuel to the speculations about a crisis in reaction to Kim Il-Song's incapacitation or even death. They pointed out a growing tension within the military over the collapse of the North Korean economy. A Chinese official stressed, Kim Jong-Il is so disliked by the Army that he "won't last a day" once Kim Il-Song dies.

Other knowledgeable foreign observers with lengthy experience in Pyongyang, mainly Russians, Iranians, and Japanese, have similar though less alarming interpretations for the sudden troop movements around Pyongyang. Having been conditioned for decades to fierce loyalty to the Kims, the Army is essentially incapable of even contemplating a military coup. But internal struggles over the redistribution of power are already taking place and are bound to escalate the moment Kim Il-Song dies. Most, however, believe that the troop movements are a precautionary measure by Kim Jong-Il.

Meanwhile, as these major movements of KPA units and forces were taking place, the KPA High Command was quietly completing yet another phase in the modernization of the forces along the DMZ, further improving them for the future assault on the South. A large number of 240mm MBRLs and 170+mm SPGs were transferred from strategic stockpiles in the rear of the DPRK to underground shelters close to the DMZ. The headquarters of Combat Command Corps were reinforced and, in effect, activated.

In late July 1993, there were new signs of a consolidation of Kim Jong-Il's power. In one article in *NoDong Sinmun*, Dr. Pak Mun-Kon even referred to a completed succession process. "Today our People's Army and people are defending the socialist stronghold, steel-strong under the leadership of the Dear Comrade Leader, an iron-willed and sagacious general, who succeeded to the *Juche* cause, pioneered by the Great Leader, and is brilliantly consummating it."

A growing emphasis on subjects important to Kim Jong-Il in the party media at this time, further reflects his growing power in Pyongyang. Indeed, locally made weapon systems dominated the major military parade in Pyongyang on 27 July 1993.

July 27, 1993, the 40th anniversary to the end of the Korean War, the DPRK's "2nd Great Victory," served as a major event devoted to rejuvenation on the basis of achievements of the past. The generally conservative and bland celebration of this major anniversary in the DPRK's revolutionary myth could not conceal a very interesting event with direct bearing on the succession process: The return of Kim Yong-Chu, Kim Il-Song's brother, to the forefront of political activities and high profile in several major events in Pyongyang.

Kim Yong-Chu was the original successor to Kim Il-Song, before the rise of Kim Jong-Il in the early 1970s. He disappeared in 1975 into a total political limbo. His life was spared just because he was the Great Leader's brother. On July 27, Kim Yong-Chu was named almost 10th in the Pyongyang hierarchy, described as a "former" holder of various titles and senior positions. No explanation was given for his return.

Observers speculated that the return of Kim Yong-Chu was associated with the apprehension of many of the Pyongyang "old guard" that Kim Il-Song's death would result in a massive purge of the older generation. The return of the younger Kim Yong-Chu to prominence may serve as a form of calming down the old guard that there won't be a clear cut and drastic generational change of guard in Pyongyang.

Indeed, as of mid August, there was a sudden resurgence of a propaganda blitz. All over the media, there were urgings for a wartime-type of sacrifice in order to ensure the survival of North Korean society. "Now we are living in a grave period, taking the destiny of socialism on our two shoulders. ... Let us struggle in a revolutionary way like in the wartime and postwar period and bring about a great upsurge in socialist economic construction." There is a preoccupation with the theme that abuses of socialism are intolerable, and demands that each citizen in the entire population is responsible for complete faith in and dedication to Kim Il-Song and Kim Jong-Il.

This propaganda campaign's old fashioned style is revealing. The unabashed return to "basics" of the late 1940s and 1950s, is aimed at the remnants of the old guard in Pyongyang rather than at the masses. With the country increasingly adopting the priorities and themes associated with Kim Jong-Il and his younger followers, the old guard have clearly become apprehensive about the pace of reforms and the extent of their power. It was therefore essential to appease them, in action through the return of Kim Yong-Chu, and in symbolism in the form of the new "old" propaganda blitz. Despite their influence, the Pyongyang old guard is not in position to challenge, let alone block, the rise to power of Kim Jong-Il and the younger generation.

23

ALMOST THERE, BUT NOT YET...

Thus, despite the sporadic public parading of Kim Il-Song in recent months, it is increasingly apparent that Kim Jong-Il is already effectively the DPRK's leader. Still, Pyongyang seems incapable of making the final and overt transfer of power from the Great Leader to the Dear Leader.

By the summer of 1993, the transition of power to Kim Jong-Il has accelerated markedly but nevertheless remained seemingly inconclusive. This is because despite a decade of preparations and half-measures, Pyongyang is nevertheless dreading the moment when the Great Leader steps off the stage leaving behind the Dear Leader in control.

This crucial phase comes at a dangerous time for the DPRK, when the threat of collapse due to severe economic crisis is not inconceivable. Kim Jong-Il inherits an unstable North Korea that must virtually abandon the *Juche* doctrine in order to survive. Under such conditions, Kim Il-Song might still decide to lash out and strike for the last time, launching the "revolutionary offensive" that is "our party's traditional struggle method." Kim Jong-Il's declaration of the "Semi-War State" and the growing preoccupation with nuclear weapons and ballistic missiles clearly demonstrates that the "Sacred War for Reunification," is very much on Pyongyang's short list of options for confronting the crises ahead.

North Korea planned to finally complete the transfer of power in the course of the General Congress of the Workers' Party then scheduled for December 1993. This will be the first Party congress since October 1980. The selection of delegates had just begun.

The climax of the Congress should be the unanimous election of Kim Jong-Il as General Secretary of the Workers' Party, a position now held by Kim Il-Song. Although Kim Jong-Il has accumulated numerous titles and power positions over the last year, this would be his most important Party related title. General Secretary of the Workers' Party is an ideological title that complements Kim Jong-Il's April appointment as Chairman of the National Defense Committee, essentially North Korea's Commander in Chief and the most important state power position.

Whether or not the General Congress actually takes place, the mere preoccupation with the election of Kim Jong-Il as General Secretary shows the priority of the succession process in North Korea.

In the last week of October 1993, there was a sudden revival of the succession issue in the North Korean media.

On October 26, virtually all the organs of the official media included the following statement in their editorials: "The Korean revolution is dynamically advancing because the question of inheriting leadership has been successfully solved and the Korean people have an illustrious head of the party and the revolution." Kim Il-Song was cited specifically confirming that Kim Jong-Il has already been the leader of North Korea for some time. "As Comrade Kim Jong-Il has wisely guided the party, the state, and the Army as a whole from long ago, the question of inheritance of leadership has been solved." Pyongyang went further to stress that "Kim Jong-Il [is] at the head of the party, the revolution, and the Revolutionary Armed Forces." Pyongyang anticipates new triumphs with Kim Jong-Il "leading our revolution."

The next day, the DPRK media further elaborated on the position of Kim Jong-Il as the country's leader. Kim Il-Song was quoted as stressing that "Comrade Kim Jong-Il is wisely leading the revolution and construction with his extraordinary ability." Virtually all the official media in Pyongyang recounted the achievements of Kim Jong-Il in building the North Korean society and economy. Until late October, such accolades were reserved solely for Kim Il-Song.

Simultaneously, Pyongyang also reported on Kim Il-Song's renewed interest in the restoration of the tomb of King Wang Kong, one of the founders of the first unified state of Korea, as a huge scale theme park. It should be remembered that between late December 1992 and mid January 1993, there had been daily coverage of Kim Il-Song's interest in the reconstruction of the Tomb of King Tongmyong, which was interpreted as a preoccupation with his own mortality, and resulted in rumors of his deteriorating health. Naturally, the reporting of his interest in another royal tomb further fueled such rumors.

On November 10, an intense campaign was launched throughout the North Korean elite to study the leadership qualities of Kim Jong-Il and vow "unquestioned trust" in him. Pyongyang's media closely covered these events, typically reporting the official position toward Kim Jong-Il: "Our people's trust in the Dear Leader Comrade Kim Jong-Il is the purest and most noble ideological feeling of entrusting all destinies entirely to the leader, an unshakable faith based on a deep understanding of the greatness of his feats and an unquestioned belief that they can [reach] their destiny when they follow the leader." Several special conferences and seminars to study the "greatness" of Kim Jong-Il were held in the next few days in the key institutions in Pyongyang.

Most important was the November 11 seminar held by the Ministry of the People's Armed Forces. Significant, the main speech was delivered by the Chief of the General Staff, Choe Kwang. Although a Kim Il-Song devotee, Choe Kwang proved himself a key supporter of Kim Jong-Il in several military and political forums. A few other senior generals delivered speeches and lectures that in effect identified Kim Jong-Il as the nation's leader. Virtually all the speeches in this seminar were concluded by a reference to Kim Jong-Il as "a great leader of people who has personified all traits of the leader of the revolution at the highest level." To date, the title "Great Leader" had been solely reserved for Kim Il-Song.

Moreover, the Minister of Defense, O Chin-U, was not mentioned as having delivered an obligatory speech or even being present in this important seminar. The omission of O Chin-U might hint at his being eased out of office with Choe Kwang emerging as a compromise leader of the Armed Forces because of his acceptability to both the old and the young guard.

There were ominous warnings of an impending major crisis. The speech of Choe Kwang asserted that Kim Jong-Il is capable of delivering "historical victory" for the DPRK by "smashing the frantic moves of the enemies." However, Choe Kwang explained, the true "greatness" of Kim Jong-Il lies in his ability to transform "a misfortune into a blessing and adversity into a favorable condition" despite the enormity of the challenges.

Meanwhile, in mid November, the DPRK suddenly raised the level of pressure on Japan. The excuse was correcting a historical wrong. Historians and experts in Pyongyang announced their discovery that the 1905 Ulsa Five-point Treaty, signed by Korean Emperor Kojong and Tokyo, which had started a Japanese 40-year rule of Korea, was "illegal." Therefore, they argued, Japan's colonialism was illegal. Pyongyang demanded huge amounts of money from Tokyo as compensation for 40 years of illegal exploitation of Korea. This rapidly raised the level of threat to Japan and at the same time, it was used an explanation to the North Korean people for why Japan should be brought into the circle of enemies, so that threats in a future war are understood and supported by the masses.

Pyongyang also cited Japan's refusal to change the name of the Sea of Japan to the Sea of East Korea as a proof of Japan's continued ill wishes toward Korea, and Tokyo's desire to renew the expansionist policy into, and ultimately control over, the Korean Peninsula. Consequently, in late November, the DPRK was already speaking openly about Tokyo's "policy hostile to the DPRK." Japan was urged to "renounce" this attitude or face the consequences. Pyongyang stressed the immediate objective of Japan, in collaboration with the ROK and the US, is to isolate the DPRK and bring about its collapse.

Meanwhile, the personality cult of Kim Jong-Il continued to grow. In mid November, there was a sharp escalation in the building of his image as a military genius, uniquely qualified to save the country. Pyongyang explained what kind of threats Kim Jong-Il would have to address, including warnings that South Korea was amassing weapons for an imminent war against the North.

Pyongyang also warned the US that it was actively preparing for withstanding sanctions and even for waging a total war over the demanded inspections of its nuclear facilities. "When we declared our decision to withdraw from the Nuclear Non-Proliferation Treaty, we had taken into account all possible consequences, and we are fully prepared to safeguard the sovereignty of the country even if 'sanctions' or war are imposed on us," Pyongyang announced, "If the US thinks pressure can work on the DPRK, it is a miscalculation...Our people and the People's Army will never yield to pressure."

On 9 and 10 December 1993, Iran and North Korea signed a major strategic agreement aimed at significantly enhancing Iran's ability to withstand a major nuclear war, presumably with the United States.

On 6 December, a large Iranian military delegation led by Defense Minister Muhammad Forouzandeh had arrived in Pyongyang for high level discussions.

The Iranian delegation included the heads of Iran's military industries, weapons procurement agencies, and the senior scientists involved in the ballistic missiles, nuclear and unconventional weapons programs. The declared objective of the delegation's visit was to attend an inter-governmental committee meeting on economic, scientific and technological cooperation. This committee serves as a front for the joint development of strategic weapons.

In the next few days, Forouzandeh held lengthy discussions with his North Korean counterpart, Marshal O Chin-U. Forouzandeh also met Yi Song-Tae, who is responsible for North Korea's external economic relations, reflecting the major financial magnitude of the anticipated agreement.

On 9 December, the two sides signed minutes of their fifth joint committee that amounted to a major strategic deal. On the next day, the details of the agreement were presented to senior officials closely associated with Kim Il-Song and Kim Jong-Il who gave their blessing, thus, in effect ratifying the strategic agreement for Pyongyang. The agreement has two main points:

1. The joint development of a new generation of ballistic missiles (with ranges between 1,500 and 3,000kms) to be produced in Iran, modified for nuclear and other warheads. This deal follows an agreement signed back in mid-March 1993 by Brig.Gen. Hussayn Mantiqe'i, the senior officer responsible for Iranian ballistic missile development and production, to acquire the *NoDong-1* and *NoDong-2* ballistic missiles, as well as production line technologies.

2. North Korean experts will build underground bunkers, primarily for production and launch of air-

craft and missiles, in some 18 sites throughout Iran, to be able to withstand American nuclear strikes, tailored after North Korea's own underground facilities

Other projects discussed by the two delegations include the development of electronic equipment and up-grading older Soviet and Chinese aircraft. In return, Iran will supply North Korea with hard currency, cheap oil, as well as access to Western technology, primarily dual-use items (such as computers) acquired in Western Europe and the Far East.

Meanwhile, in late November, Pyongyang urged the entire Korean people to prepare for a new wave of revolutionary revitalization that will take Korea to new levels of achievements. Everybody in North Korea was preparing for the dawn of a new era. A new song , "Our Father is Marshal Kim Jong-II", was already being taught in kindergartens and schools in preparations for a new personality cult wave.

24

THE WINTER OF TURMOIL

In early December 1993, there were drastic changes in the top level of the WPK. Most important was the reinstatement of Kim Yong-Ju, Kim Il-Song's younger brother, first as member of the Politburo and then as a Vice-President. These last minute maneuvers are a way to persuade the remnants of the older guard, fiercely loyal to Kim Il-Song, that the rise of the young Kim Jong-Il will not harm their power and privilege.

To further strengthen the position of Kim Jong-Il, Pyongyang enlarged the family circle around him. For example, Kim Jong-Il's half brother, Kim Pyong-Il, was recalled to Pyongyang from Bulgaria, where he was serving as ambassador, in effect exiled. His mother, Kim Song-Ae, was also brought back from obscurity to head North Korea's Women's League. Huang Chang-Yop, an ideologist and arch-conservative who is married to one of Kim Il-Song's nieces, was elected the chairman of the foreign affairs committee, an oversight position over the DPRK's foreign affairs. These family appointments are actually efforts by Kim Il-Song to help Kim Jong-Il complete the succession.

The return of Kim Pyong-Il to Pyongyang is even more significant. According to material provided by KPA Capt. Shin Chung-Chol, Kim Pyong-Il is now the military confidante of Kim Jong-Il and the primary source of wholly trusted military advice. Capt. Shin is a former classmate of Kim Pyong-Il. Kim Pyong-Il told Shin that his own anticipated future role is supporting his half brother, Kim Jong-Il, as a senior commander especially during major challenges such as a new Korean war. In order to better prepare for this task, Kim Pyong-Il was sent to Eastern Europe in the early 1980s to absorb the latest military and strategic knowledge from Soviet and Warsaw Pact experts. His position as the DPRK ambassador to Sofia was a cover for military and intelligence activities.

There were other meaningful changes in the Pyongyang elite. Along with Kim Yong-Ju, Kim Pyong-Sik was nominated second vice president. Kim Pyong-Sik is a very intriguing selection. He is the chairman of the Social Democratic Party of North Korea. He had stayed in Japan and was educated there. He was active in subverting and organizing the local Korean community. Between 1966 and 1972, he served as deputy chairman of *Chosen Soren*, the residents' association and a major source of "contributions" of foreign currency. His goal is to bring about the recovery of North Korean economy through the inducement of foreign investment from Japanese and other Pacific Rim sources.

Also, Hong Sok-Hyong was nominated new chief of economic planning. His and Kim Pyong-Sik's nomination are part of an overall change in government as a result of an overall economic failure too severe to conceal. Indeed, food and fuel shortages became so acute that people in rural areas were being encouraged to eat two rather than three meals a day, and even in Pyongyang such elementary things as hot water were in short supply. The shortages in electricity had direct impact on the working hours of non-essential factories.

Indeed, in early December, the WPK admitted that since the collapse of the communist bloc, the DPRK has been forced to pay world prices for essential imports. "This has not only caused serious damage to our economic construction, but has also made it inevitable to adjust the pace and balance of our overall economic development and made it impossible to fulfill the Third Seven-Year Plan as scheduled." The WPK elaborated further, that these economic failures had a direct impact on the standard of living of all North Koreans. Pyongyang then emphasized that in principle, the economic crisis justified the need to confront the enemy and prepare for unification by force. "Faced with the increasing danger of a new war on the Korean Peninsula, we have had to direct many things in the economic field to national defense in order to strengthen the nation's defense capabilities."

Technocrats are on the decline while people in the military are on the rise, taking over positions usually reserved for civilians. Meanwhile, the retention of members of the old guard ensures that ideological purity is not infringed upon.

It is noteworthy that the most recent phase of personality cult centers on Kim Jong-Il's ability as the Supreme Commander of the armed forces and his preparations for the forthcoming crisis. "The cause of continuously strengthening and developing the revolutionary armed forces in our country is being brilliantly realized by the Dear Leader Comrade Kim Jong-Il [who has] turned the entire ranks into iron-strong revolutionary soldiers and ensured that the combat capability and arms and equipment of the People's Army are strengthened continuously."

In order to reinforce this message, over the next few days, several symposium discussions devoted to Kim Jong-Il's "Greatness" were held all over the country. The emphasis was again on trust in his ability to lead the nation through to the ultimate triumph.

In countless radio broadcasts, articles and pamphlets, particularly distributed among KPA personnel and potential reservists, Kim Jong-Il was hailed as "a great military genius and iron-willed brilliant commander" who will be able to overcome any adversity. "His traits as a great brilliant commander lie also in matchless grit and iron will not wavering before any thunder and lightning." The KPA troops were reminded that they "trust and follow [Kim Jong-Il] as their destiny" and especially that they see him as the only one capable of liberating the South. Over the next few days, the propaganda campaign accelerated, stressing the unity between the commander and the people.

The priorities of Kim Jong-Il's KPA, most notably, military modernization and the introduction of new weapon systems, were clearly explained in an article by KPA Colonel Han Po. "What is important in the leadership of Kim Jong-Il is that he is steadily increasing the military technical might of the People's Army in every way." Colonel Han Po stressed that on top of Kim Jong-Il's ideological achievements, "he has founded a powerful defense industry suitable to the demand of modern warfare and turned the whole country into an impregnable fortress."

Pyongyang emphasized an escalating crises with both the ROK and the US. The current emphasis is on the "semi-war state" originally declared by Kim Jong-Il in 1993, which is considered his first real test of major military responsibility. "Because of the reckless war commotion and aggressive maneuvers of the imperialists, the danger of a war did not disappear at all in our country and there was a dangerous touch-and-go situation. Nevertheless, the Dear Leader Comrade Kim Jong-Il, our Supreme Commander, led our revolutionary armed force, making it possible for us to repeatedly achieve victory in the acute military and political confrontation where the enemy's guns and shells were not fired."

Pyongyang presents the "semi-war state" as a key event in which the KPA was able to deter infringement of DPRK sovereignty. The KPA "consistently and vigorously stepped forward during this semi-state-of-war period and did not allow the enemies to touch even one inch of land or a single blade of grass. Today they are fully prepared for combat mobilization."

A major speech by Vice Marshal Choe Kwang, refrained from openly acknowledging the nuclear capabilities of the DPRK. However, he clearly addresses the subject in the indirect manner that is characteristic of Communist writings. "The fact that we crushed the enemy's vicious challenges during the semi-war period and again displayed the fatherland's dignity and honor throughout the world was the proud victory of the might of our single-minded unity more powerful than atomic bombs. We will win victory eternally in the future on the strength of our single-minded unity around the respected and beloved Comrade Supreme Commander. The respected and beloved Comrade Supreme Commander, with clairvoyant and extraordinary wisdom, has scientifically penetrated the characteristics of modern wars and has strengthened the special arms unit of the KPA and has seen to it that the armed equipment of the KPA should be further modernized."

Vice Marshal Choe Kwang anticipates a major improvement in the power of the KPA, and the DPRK as a whole, under Kim Jong-Il. "The era of Kim Jong-Il when we will march under the leadership of the respected and beloved Comrade Supreme Commander, even though today is still an honorable era, will become a brighter, more prosperous era in the future." The role of the KPA in this bright era is to finally realize their country's sacred goal, unification of the Korean Peninsula by force. "Today, our People's Army has the heavy and honorable task of re unifying the fatherland with guns in the nineties without fail and completing the *Juche* revolutionary cause, the socialist cause, to the end."

Choe Kwang stressed that military might is the key to unification: "If we are to complete the *Juche* revolutionary cause, cultivated by the Great Leader, to the end, we must strengthen the People's Army, the party's revolutionary armed forces, by all means. Only when we strengthen the People's Army, can we crush all challenges of the enemy and firmly guarantee the honorable Kim Jong-Il era."

The anticipation of a major crisis was further stressed in Kim Il-Song's new year's speech on January 1st, 1994. He sounded moderate and restrained when compared to the military drum beatings coming out of Pyongyang. However, on a closer look, Kim Il-Song predicted a new Korean War.

Kim Il-Song started with the DPRK's desire for unification. However, he went on, as long as the "fascist regime" in Seoul is in power, not only will national reconciliation prove impossible to accomplish, but "it would result only in confrontation and war between the fellow countrymen." Kim Il-Song stressed that "Pressure or threat will have no effect on us. Such an attempt may invite catastrophe, far from finding a solution to the problem." Kim Il-Song also had a special warning to the US. "The United States must see all the facts squarely and behave with prudence." Otherwise, he warned, the US will be solely responsible for the "grave consequences" of its actions in front of the whole world.

Kim Il-Song's warnings were soon reflected in feverish action. On January 12, a high-level KPA Air Force delegation led by Air Force Commander Cho Myong-Nok left for Tehran to discuss strategic cooperation as well as study the military capabilities and posture of the Iranians. On that day, Tehran stressed the growing importance of forming "strong and effective alliance" of like-minded states in order to resist and withstand the imminent war with the US. Tehran is convinced that war is inevitable because Washington cannot tolerate the global strategic ramifications of the rise and spread of Islam. Therefore, Tehran advocated "forming an alliance" based on "clear and genuine political strategy." The negotiations with the North Koreans would center on these issues.

Thus, in mid January, the DPRK and Iran engaged in high-level negotiations in Tehran on "the development of new weapon systems, including medium- and long-range missiles." Air Force Commander Cho Myong-Nok and the North Korean delegation reached Tehran on January 15 and were met by Muhsin Reza'i. The DPRK delegation also included the commander of the artillery and strategic forces, as well as 28 senior officers, missile experts and nuclear scientists. It is the highest military delegation ever to visit a non-communist country. Ultimately, the North Korean delegation remained in Iran for a whole month, in itself an indication of the importance of the strategic-military negotiations.

The two delegations discussed strategic issues of the highest level and reached agreements on such issues as nuclear weapons and jointly going to war against the US. Early on, the military leaders needed the approval of their respective civilian political leaderships for the agreements reached because they were that crucial. Therefore, in late January, Manuchehr Mottaki, the Deputy Foreign Minister of Iran for Legal Affairs, suddenly left for Pyongyang for discussions with Yang Hyong-Sop, the Speaker of the DPRK Assembly. Ostensibly they were discussing the expansion of parliamentarian cooperation. In reality, they were dealing with a politically important legal issue concerning joint cooperation that had arisen during the discussions in Tehran. The strategic discussions were completed successfully soon afterwards.

Meanwhile, the Iranian-North Korean discussions

also covered the development and production in Iran of the NK-SCUD-C and the *NoDong-2*. "The new missiles can carry chemical and nuclear warheads and hit almost any Middle Eastern capital." They also discussed the resumption of their joint SSM testing program in Iran. The joint missile porogram now includes 800 North Korean experts working in Iran, and over 50 Iranians in North Korea.

Meanwhile, the "crowning" of Kim Jong-Il, widely anticipated for December 1993, was postponed by Pyongyang in order not to associate the new leader with the acknowledgment of the major economic crisis. Indeed, North Korea has embarked on a series of attempts to markedly improve such issues as the basic food and fuel supplies. Food, mainly basic cereal, is purchased from the West, including the United States, on humanitarian grounds and as part of the bribery for Pyongyang's agreement to allow the IAEA inspection. Additional supplies of fuel, originally Iraqi oil, transferred via Iran, are being delivered in return for additional weapons and strategic cooperation. It is noteworthy that even before this new deal, Iran was already the source of 40% of the DPRK's oil.

Knowledgeable sources in Pyongyang, mainly veteran diplomats and other foreign officials, now expected Kim Jong-Il to officially assume power on 16 February 1994. This is a very symbolic date for Kim Jong-Il because he joined the WPK in February 1964, and the WPK was notified formally and publicly of his nomination to succeed Kim Il-Song in February 1974, (although he was first mentioned as heir in September 1973 in a closed session). Reportedly, the WPK Central Committee decided to postpone the "crowning" in order to mark the 30th and 20th anniversaries of Kim Jong-Il's rise to power, as well as commemorate his 52nd birthday. It is more likely, however, that Pyongyang wanted to pass through the current economic crisis without having to deal with the power transfer at the same time.

Meanwhile, irrespective of the IAEA inspection crisis, the overall crisis between North Korea and the West is bound to intensify. The main reason is that the DPRK would like to isolate itself as much as possible for the period of the final and formal hand over of power from Kim Il-Song to Kim Jong-Il. Pyongyang prefers to have the undivided attention of the ruling elite devoted to this crucial day in the life of the DPRK, and as little outside interference in the process as possible. A major international crisis will inevitably reduce the presence of foreigners and their economic activities to a bare minimum, as well as justify the expulsion of foreigners who would not leave on their own. As for the possibility of such a crisis escalating into a major war, Pyongyang is convinced that it firmly controls the initiative.

PART IV

END GAME

The overall crisis between North Korea and the West is bound to intensify—irrespective of the ostensible resolution of the IAEA inspection crisis—simply because Pyongyang is determined to isolate itself for the period of the final and formal hand over of power from Kim Il-Song to Kim Jong-Il. Therefore, the crisis and tension will continue to grow irrespective of the extent of compromises reached by the United States and South Korea. Western economic "incentives," the politically correct euphomism for paying ransom, will always be welcome in the impoverished DPRK, but will not affect the decision-making process. Pyongyang desperately needs an international crisis to ensure that the undivided attention of the ruling elite is indeed devoted to this crucial day in the life of the DPRK.

Thus, the need to rely on an external crisis, and possibly war, in order to ensure the completion of the succession process in Pyongyang, increases as the hand-over of power is essentially completed. Despite the sporadic public parading of Kim Il-Song in recent months, it is increasingly apparent that Kim Jong-Il is already effectively the DPRK's leader. Still, Pyongyang seems incapable of making the final and overt transfer of power from the Great Leader to the Dear Leader.

25

CRISIS

Since the fall of 1993, the transition of power to Kim Jong-Il continues to accelerate dramatically but nevertheless remains rather smooth and, seemingly, inconclusive. This is because Pyongyang is in trepidations of that dreaded moment when the Great Leader steps off the stage leaving behind Dear Leader in control. This fear exists despite a decade of preparations and half-measures. This is the price of the Kims' personality cult.

Moreover, this crucial phase comes at a most dangerous time to the DPRK, when the threat of collapse due to severe economic crisis is not inconceivable. Kim Jong-Il inherits an unstable North Korea that must virtually abandon the *Juche* doctrine to survive. Under such conditions, Kim Il-Song might still decide to lash out and strike for the last time, launching the "revolutionary offensive" that is "our party's traditional struggle method."

The DPRK desperately needs an international crisis in order to consolidate its power structure. With their country on the brink of the sacred war of unification, and perhaps even a nuclear war, the KPA High Command and the national defense elite will inevitably rally behind the supreme leader of the day, be it Kim Il-Song or Kim Jong-Il, in order to realize their country's manifest destiny. The support of the DPRK's Armed Forces is considered crucial for the survival of the Kims' regime. Back in the spring of 1993, a high level North Korean defector predicted that after Kim Il-Song's death, with the military "supporting Kim Jong-Il...North Korea could keep its system [of government] for ever." A major crisis would be a failsafe way to secure the loyalty of the military establishment. Indeed, a major war may very well seem a tempting solution to all North Korea's troubles.

It should be remembered that since mid 1992, Pyongyang has in effect been issuing the West an ultimatum: either bail out the North Korean economy and finance its modernization or North Korea will strike out against South Korea and Japan, shattering the stability of the entire Pacific Rim. Indeed, a senior North Korean official acknowledged already in June 1992 that "North Korea may end up taking a certain type of military action for its survival if [the] superpowers support only one side."

The tension along the Korean DMZ reached unprecedented heights already in the fall of 1993. The North Korean Armed Forces are mobilized and reinforced in forward positions optimal for the launching of a surprise attack on South Korea. In early November 1993, Pyongyang ordered the shaving off of the hair of all its military personnel and eligible reservists, improving their chances of surviving exposure to chemical and biological weapons. Such extreme steps are considered to be indications of last minute preparations for war.

Pyongyang is confident in its ability to dominate the crisis in the Korean Peninsula because their whole society is based on a purely offensive military scenario. Pyongyang envisions triumph within 7 days of the outbreak of war. Within this time they plan to neutralize the bulk of US/ROK forces near the DMZ, derail Korean mobilization and the arrival of US reinforcements, occupy Seoul, and then bring South Korea to the point of demanding cease fire and peace negotiations. It is highly likely that chemical weapons will be used in the offensive. Of great importance is the contribution of the tens of thousands of special forces and terrorists, already in South Korea, expected to be activated in the rear of the ROK, opening a "second front" as destructive to US/ROK forces as the main front. Although Pyongyang expects a total victory in a short war, there is clear willingness and readiness to complete the mission throughout a long war and at any price.

Under present conditions, from a pure military perspective, this short war scenario has a good chance to succeed, especially if the United States delays its reaction to the North Korean aggression.

It is toward this end that the North Korean nuclear arsenal of at least 6 weapons, at least 4 of which are 50kt warheads mounted on NK-SCUDs and *NoDong*-type ballistic missiles, was acquired. The primary objective of this arsenal is to provide Pyongyang with the means to issue a credible nuclear ultimatum, for any one of these nuclear-tipped ballistic missiles can cause tremendous amounts of casualties and damage to an urban center. The guidance systems of these missiles, based on Western high-technology proven so effective during the Gulf War, enables the North Koreans to reliably aim their missiles at key sectors of target-cities.

At the very least, deliberations in Washington on the appropriate reaction to the North Korean invasion and the nuclear threat will provide the KPA enough time to complete the short war scenario encirclement of the Korean Peninsula.

Former KPA officers who defected recently portray an even more chilling scenario involving the possible use of the DPRK's few nuclear weapons, "As a preemptive strike, North Korea would attack US military bases in Japan and then launch air raids on Japan's major military bases."

In case Pyongyang decides to expand the ultimatum to include a direct threat to the United States itself, it would most likely do so with cruise missiles fitted with biological-weapon warheads. A credible threat would be a warning to launch one or more of these missiles against a coastal metropolitan center such as New York, Atlanta, Los Angeles, or even Washington DC. The DPRK is known to have seaborne cruise missiles that can be launched from trawlers and cargo ships, or converted civilian vessels camouflaged under the flags of neutral countries. There should be no doubt that if such terror weapons are utilized, Washington will react with fury, essentially obliterating the DPRK. The real danger, however, lies in the mere North Korean threat to use such weapons, which would no doubt lead to the delay of a US reaction allowing the completion of North Korea's short-war scenario.

The KPA High Command is very confident about

the outcome of the future war in Korea. In early December 1993, DPRK Deputy Defense Minister, Vice Marshal Kim Guan-Chzhin, warned that Seoul was pushing the peninsula toward war. He stressed the quality of the KPA and their ability to soundly defeat the South. A war, Vice Marshal Kim Guan-Chzhin threatened, will be Seoul's "fatal mistake." Russian military analysts share his confidence. They emphasize that Seoul bases its entire defense on the presence of the US nuclear umbrella. However, the existence of a North Korean nuclear ultimatum may very well neutralize the Americans leaving the South at the mercy of the KPA's non-nuclear forces. It is noteworthy that the US currently has no nuclear weapons in South Korea.

The North Korean military buildup comes at a the same time as Pyongyang finds itself under extreme pressure as a result of a collapsing economy and the completion of the transfer of power from Kim Il-Song to Kim Jong-Il. Pyongyang sees the initiation of a major crisis as a means of solidifying the support of the all important military elite by clearly demonstrating that the "Sacred War for Reunification" is very much a priority.

26

KIM JONG-IL AS LEADER

Insecurity in Pyongyang over the succession of Kim Jong-Il has resulted in the postponement of the final "crowning". Knowledgeable sources in Pyongyang expected Kim Jong-Il to officially assume power on 16 February 1994. When it finally occurs, it will only increase the pressure in Pyongyang for a dramatic breakout from the current economic collapse. It will be incumbent upon the new leader and the younger elite to quickly prove their right to power. With an economic recovery within the framework of their traditional ideology virtually impossible, a major military crisis is the only viable option for Pyongyang to consolidate the power of the new regime. With the stakes so high, it is most likely that such a crisis will escalate into a major war , the new Korean War.

In early February 1994, there were reports about a possibility of last minute changes in the succession process in Pyongyang. The source was Kim Yong-Chu, the newly promoted young brother of Kim Il-Song, who talked to an East European friend on his way to Beijing. "There will be no final transfer of power to Kim Jong-Il as long as Kim Il-Song lives," Kim Yong-Chu was quoted as saying. Kim Jong-Il remains the undisputed "crown prince" and he is in total control over "domestic affairs." However, Kim Yong-Chu stressed, Kim Il-Song suddenly insists on making key decisions concerning "foreign policy" such as the current crisis with the US. Ever since the final phase of the succession process began, the possibility of Kim Il-Song's insisting on a last personal attempt at unification of the Korean Peninsula was a dominant factor in determining the final hand over of power to Kim Jong-Il.

A possible further complication in the Pyongyang succession was raised on 17 February 1994 when Lee Ki-Taek, South Korea's main opposition leader, claimed that he had been told by an American official that Kim Jong-Il had sustained serious but unspecified injuries. "I heard Kim Jong-Il was so critically injured that he would not be able to carry out his official duties if he took power," Lee said. "I do not know whether the injuries were from a traffic accident or from a shooting," he added. "But it does not seem to be from natural causes." These rumors were denied by Pyongyang as "totally groundless," and also by officials in Seoul and Beijing but the fact remains that Kim Jong-Il was last seen in public on 9 December 1993. Significantly, he missed his own elaborate 52nd birthday celebrations.

However, other evidence strongly suggests that Kim Jong-Il is still at the helm. As of 17 February, Pyongyang has even been stressing Kim Jong-Il's growing preparations for the reunification of the Korean peninsula. For example, Radio Pyongyang reported that "Kim Jong-Il is giving guidance to overall state and party affairs and, with his exceptional interest in the reunification issue, is leading the entire nation on the road of reunification."

While the rumors of an assassination attempt proved "groundless," Kim Jong-Il did suffer some brain damage in September 1993. He was in a traffic accident, and crashed his car while speeding—probably while intoxicated. According to Chinese military medical experts, including senior brain surgeons, Kim Jong-Il even suffered damage to the bones in his skull. These injuries come on top of a severe head injury Kim Jong-Il suffered around June 1993 as a result of falling off a horse.

The Chinese experts suggest that as a consequence of these cumulative head injuries Kim Jong-Il suffers from "a serious desease of his psychoneurotic system." A Chinese official went even further to point out that: "It has been indirectly confirmed that it is almost impossible for Kim Jong-Il to recieve foreign guests or carry out official work because of the worsening of his desease of the psychoneurotic system." At present, this Chinese observation is judged by Western experts to be far more severe than the actual case. Still, the mental state of Kim Jong-Il is a reason for apprehension.

Western medical experts suggest that such a succession of blows to the brain may result in the dropping of brain cells, early atrophy, or even some shrinking of the brain. Such a condition leads to mood swings in the affected individual. A very unstable person will display a greater tendency to fly off the handle. With time, the impairment may grow further, but the individual will not notice the change. This danger is more accute especially if the affected individual is surrounded by sycophants. Thus, the individual in question can act irrationally, especially if there is no one to restrain him. Most important, individuals so affected tend to lose a sense of continuity. They tend to concentrate on immediate actions in order to deliver immediate gratification. They gradually lose any sense of consequence and cannot anticipate the results of one's actions!

This personality and psychological profile was assembled on the basis of fragmentary medical data alone. Still, the profile fits closely the known patterns of behavior of Kim Jong-Il. This means that the irrationality, instability, and tendency to gamble will only increase in Kim Jong-Il and his Pyongyang.

Meanwhile, appehensive about these rumors, Pyongyang moved to dispel them. On 28 February, Kim Jong-Il met with Ho Chong-Man, the Vice-Chairman of the Japanese *Chongyon* —the General Association of Korean Residents of Japan (an organization that channels tremendous amounts of foreign currency, food, and forbidden high technology to the DPRK). They even had dinner together. Then, on 5 March, Kim Jong-Il finally appeared in public in his capacity as the KPA Supreme Commander. He attended a special Army song and dance show about the importance and inevitability of the unification by force of the Korean Peninsula.

Meanwhile, Kim Jong-Il maintains his usual daily schedule. He works until very late, usually the predawn hours, and then sleeps late. During the day he makes frequent breaks in the work schedule to recieve "special treatment and enjoyment" from a "pleassuregiving team" under close and specific medical supervision. He also continues to watch foreign movies specially imported from the West for his enjoyment and that of his close cronies.

Most important are the many late night sessions in which Kim Jong-Il and a few of his most trusted loyalists debate key issues while enjoying the company of pretty women. Well informed Japanese sources believe that the question of initiating a war with South Korea has been raised in these sessions over the last year. The discussion between Kim Jong-Il and his confidants reached the point of contemplating specific scenarios for provoking a major military clash with the South. Talk included conducting an audacious act of terrorism and even launching a surprise attack and a major regional war.

Moreover, since he assumed responsibilities for defense and foreign affairs, Kim Jong-Il has developed a unique "reception-center political style"—the equivalent of an informal kitchen cabinet—made up of a few loyalists and confidants whom he trusts most. It is noteworthy that he includes mainly technocrats, experts, military people, scientists, and other professionals whose expertise can support state affairs. Kim Jong-Il clearly values their knowledge and abilities. Their late night discussions are reportedly conducted in a relatively relaxed environment that promotes the free exchange of opinion and information. Ultimately, Kim Jong-Il is being portrayed as being far less troubled by formalities, as a more open personality, and one preoccupied with substance. He does have political ability and was properly groomed for making decisions and managing crises.

However, at the very same time, these loyalists

continue to display flattery and cronyism in their relations with Kim Jong-Il. In view of Kim Jong-Il's mental condition and dangerous tendencies when free of external restraint, the question remains how free, how objective, and how effective these sessions are. Furthermore, there remains the question of Kim Jong-Il's own ability to make decisions, and especially his growing inclination towards bold gambles for immediate effect, even though risking a crisis and, even, war.

Meanwhile, there has been a slow down in the completion of the succession process. Kim Jong-Il himself now suggests that he will not be crowned until after his father's death. The reason given in Pyongyang is Kim Il-Song's determination to be the official and legal leader of the DPRK while the last effort to unify Korea by force—which means war with the ROK and US—is made. It is clear that in the meantime Kim Jong-Il continues to assume more and more power and responsibility, including preparing the DPRK for future challenges—under his own rule—and for the immediate military and nuclear crisis.

27

INSPECTIONS AND
THREATS

The imminence of a new Korean war is, at the very least, the conviction at the highest levels of power in Pyongyang. The DPRK has already designated 1995 as "the year for reunification" and several KPA officers who defected in 1992-3 confirmed that this commitment had already had a direct impact on their training. They are convinced that Pyongyang is genuinely serious about an imminent unification by force. There will be further consolidation of power by Kim Jong-Il in 1994. However, Kim Il-Song may still remain a titular head of the DPRK, at least for the grand attempt at unification. Russian military analysts estimated in early December 1993 that the greatest danger for the unleashing of hostilities on the Korean peninsula is between now and 1995.

Recently, the DPRK has elevated the intensity of its threats. On 5 February 1994, Pyongyang warned that the US was actively trying to instigate a new

Korean War "under the guise of aiming for peace on the Korean Peninsula" and threatened that the US and its allies will be defeated in such a war. "With the intention to unleash a new war in Korea, the United States is stepping up its arms build-up in and around South Korea and engaging itself in military espionage, preparing to launch a surprise strike [on North Korea]." Pyongyang vowed not to let such an attack materialize even as the danger to North Korea is increasing. "Military moves of the war-thirsty US have become all the more undisguised entering the new year." Pyongyang believes the US "will suffer a more tragic and grave defeat than in the past Korean War in which it was merely humbled and bruised all over." Pyongyang stresses that all threats are futile. "No military pressure or strong arm can ever work on the Korean people. Our people know of the vulnerability of the United States, we have the experience of fighting it for three years regarded not as a superpower but as a bluffing paper tiger."

Washington has very few options in dealing with the growing crisis in Korea. Right now, early 1994, the Clinton Administration is determined to contain the crisis and avoid war in the near term virtually at all cost. Hence, the apparent compromise with the DPRK on the single limited inspection that will not include the disputed sites that originally started the NPT dispute. The price for this compromise was very high, namely the cancellation of US military exercises that had long been a symbol of commitment to the safety and well being of the ROK.

The long awaited IAEA inspections took place in early March 1994 and, as expected, they were a sham. The North Koreans were extremely hostile to the delegation and the movements of the inspectors were restricted. They were even prevented from extracting samples from the 'hot cell' in the reactor, the only way to truly verify what the DPRK is up to. The IAEA inspectors discovered that some seals on measurement equipment left behind had been broken, but the IAEA accepted North Korean explanation that these were the results of "careless handling" by North Korean technicians.

On 18 March, Pyongyang reacted with fury to the IAEA criticism, considered by a North Korean spokesman to be "utterly unjustifiable." The IAEA presented North Korea with "unjust demands" that constituted a "flagrant violation of the Vienna agreement of February 15," in which North Korea agreed to the inspections. The DPRK warned that it would respond to further pressure with "a resolute measure." On 22 March, North Korean diplomats warned that the DPRK was considering leaving the NPT all together because of its strong anti-North Korean standing.

Meanwhile, the DPRK was raising the level of threats of war on the Korean peninsula. On 19 March, Park Young Su, North Korea's chief negotiator with South Korea, threatened war as the North Korean delegation stormed from the negotiations room at the border village of Panmunjon. Park Young Su declared that the DPRK would go to war if the world continued to pressure the DPRK into further nuclear inspections. "If you act like that, collision is inevitable and war is unavoidable," Park warned. "We are ready either for dialogue or for war." Song Young-Dae, the chief of the South Korean delegation, recalled Park's outburst. "North Korea said that Seoul was not very far from here and that it could be in flames," Song repeated. "Confrontations can spread to war. We are prepared to answer back with talks for talks or war for war."

Soon afterwards, Pyongyang demanded that South Korea, "apologize to the nation for their criminal act in having abused the exchange of special envoys ... to obstruct the [DPRK-US] talks." The next day, the DPRK increased the level of threats. Pyongyang blamed Seoul for the breakdown of talks and warned that North Korea would "take a decisive self-defensive measure" if sanctions are imposed against it. "We mean what we say," Pyongyang stressed.

On 22 March, Pyongyang warned that the US decision to deploy Patriot anti-aircraft missiles to South Korea was an aggressive act, and would lead to a regional war. "This is a provocative step to lead the situation to extremes by further aggravating tensions on the Korean peninsula. The order by Clinton to deploy Patriot missiles in South Korea is a grave threat to us. This clearly shows that the United States is leading the Korean peninsula to the situation of war." The next day, Pyongyang repeted the warning in a sterner language. North Korea called President Clinton's decision "a provocative step to drive the situation into extremes by intensifying the tensions on the Korean Peninsula." Pyongyang stressed that the deployment of any American weapon to the ROK "is a grave threat to the DPRK and it clearly shows that the United States is pushing the situation of the Korean Peninsula to the brink of war."

28

THREATS OF WAR

Meanwhile, the DPRK is constantly raising the ante. Pyongyang has made it abundantly clear that its withdrawal from the NPT was the result of careful consideration that had taken into account the possibility of a confrontation with the US resulting in sanctions and even war. There is no doubt that Pyongyang is determined to triumph through these trials. In his 1994 new year's address Kim Il-Song stated that the DPRK must intensify its preparations and readiness for the clash ahead. "This year, too, we must naturally put efforts into strengthening the country's defense power to counter the enemy's moves to provoke war." Kim Il-Song declared that the DPRK "must be fully prepared politically and ideology, militarily and materially, to deal with any contingency on our initiative."

Indeed, as of early March 1994, there has been a marked increase in Pyongyang's militaristic propaganda. There is emphasis on the KPA and the people rallying behind Kim Jong-Il for the cataclysmic confrontation with the West and the realization of the sacred unification by force. A new element was introduced on 8 March—the comparison of the current and unfolding crisis with the semi-war status of 1993. The current crisis is a direct continuation of the previous crisis. This distinction is important because the 1993 crisis was Kim Jong-Il's doing, his first true test of crisis management and decision making.

Pyongyang stressed that in this current time of crisis, the North Korean people and their Army "have the unshakable will to defend supreme commander General Kim Jong-Il with their lives forever in the future, with the same fighting spirit and stamina they displayed during the semi-war state last year. As long as there is such faithful people full of death-defying readiness to share the life and death with their Great Leader and their Dear Leader, no enemy can dare harm and provoke us."

On 10 March, Kim Jong-Il was hailed as a "great military genius" whose leadership "is a basic guarantee of all victories of the People's Army." Pyongyang issued strong suggestions that Kim Jong-Il is in direct command of military operations. Stressing the contribution of Kim Jong-Il to the modernization and war preparation of the KPA, Pyongyang emphasized that "based on the great *Juche* idea he newly elucidated systematically and on a full basis all military problems such as viewpoint on war, revolutionary armed force building, national defense construction, military strategy, and the art of commanding the Army. ... The Dear Leader Comrade Kim Jong-Il is a military genius who has boundless military insights, limitless boldness, extensive military knowledge, and political insights. He is also a great commander who has an art of military operations with which he commands all Armed Forces of the country in a unified manner and makes them act like one."

In subsequent days, there were additional articles and radio broadcasts on the "genius" of Kim Jong-Il in virtually all aspects of leadership—both at the national level and the ideological guidance of the Party. Meanwhile, as of March 10, North Korean oral propaganda—primarily a series of loudspeaker propaganda broadcasts near the DMZ—repeatedly referred to Kim Jong-Il as "president." From the context of these broadcasts, it is not yet clear whether this is a new title for Kim Jong-Il indicating another major step in the succession process, or merely an expression of "excessive loyalty" by the military group that runs these broadcasts. However, some senior South Korean officials see in these broadcasts the first indications of the imminent completion of the succession from Kim Il-Song to Kim Jong-Il. On March 23, South Korean Defence Minister Rhee Byoung-Tae stated that "there is a possibility that North Korea may name Kim Jong-Il as its president during a meeting of the People's Supreme Assembly, which starts on April 6. We are closely watching the situation."

However, preparations for what once more seemed as the final phase in the transfer of power from Kim Il-Song to Kim Jong-Il started even earlier. On 2 April, the WPK concluded a sudden 3-day conference attended by over 10,600 regional and national leaders, mainly party cell secretaries. This conference was unique in that it was the first ever summoned by Kim Jong-Il, rather than Kim Il-Song. Kim Il-Song did not attend, but send a letter that was read in the opening ceremonies. It stressed Kim Jong-Il's "excellent personality and qualities as the people's leader." Little wonder that virtually all the speaker during the conference devoted their speeches to praising the leadership qualities of Kim Jong-Il and his unique importance as an ideological leader. Many of the speakers, as well as the coverage of the conference in the North Korean media, left the impression that the final transfer of power may finally be at hand.

This kind of agitation and brain washing is so effective that, according to former high level defectors from North Korea now mainly in Russia/CIS, Kim Il-Song genuinely fears a revolt in the military if he, or Kim Jong-Il, fails to deliver the promise of war and military glory. The KPA is fully "agitated" since the semi-war incident last spring and is already showing the effects of the long period of high alert, war hysteria, and living underground in extreme conditions. The troops of the KPA know that they are enduring all of this and more for the "mythical" nuclear weapons that are the guarantors of North Korea's safety. Several defectors reaffirmed that everybody "knows" the DPRK has these weapons. For example, Sergeant Yi Chung-Kuk who defected in early March 1994 recalled that "high North Korean military officers used to encourage soldiers by saying they had nothing to fear [of the US] because the People's Army possesses nuclear arms." In view of this commitment within the ranks of the KPA, if Pyongyang surrenders to any perception of IAEA/US/ROK pressure or UN sanctions, the entire military system will snap and rebel against Pyongyang's betrayal of sacred causes and the essence of their lives.

29

THE CHINA FACTOR

Considering that the current crisis in the Korean peninsula is driven primarily by the trials and tribulations of the succession process inside Pyongyang, rather than any external impetus, then the simple fear of a military explosion, or a revolt, in the event of an unacceptable compromise may, in itself, become a decisive factor in pushing Pyongyang into taking audacious gambles and risking war with the United States.

Ultimately, economic sanctions are irrelevant. The North Korean economy is so isolated and near collapse, on its own merits, that sanctions can only have marginal impact. Moreover, the PRC, the DPRK's largest economic partner, is adamantly against the imposition of any sanctions, because Pyongyang is so crucial to Beijing's regional grand designs and underground military exports and without the active cooperation of Beijing nothing will happen.

In the spring of 1994, Beijing not only sided with Pyongyang in the mounting crisis, but moved to conduct a series of high level consultations in order to ensure joint policies. In late February, Beijing sent a major delegation to Pyongyang, ostensibly led by Li Shuzheng, the head of CPC's International Liaison Department. Actually, the delegation included many senior Party, Intelligence and Military officials who came to Pyongyang in order to discuss the crisis with the US. Li Shuzheng herself also carried invitations from President Jiang Zemin to Kim Il-Song to come to Beijing for talks about joint policies and a common approach to the upcoming crisis with the US. The Chinese also wanted to consult with the North Koreans at the highest levels possible in the aftermath of visits by American, Japanese and South Koreans officials. Kim Il-Song is expected to visit the PRC after March 1994. He will also hold very sensitive "private" discussions with Deng Xiaoping in order to affirm the special unique alliance between their two countries.

Soon afterwards, Kim Jong-Il will also visit the PRC to discuss specific issues of military technical cooperation, as well as dealing with the impending crisis and sanctions. This visit is to be used by Beijing also for a first-hand evaluation of the mental capacity of Kim Jong-Il. If successful, Kim Jong-Il's visit is expected to constitute a demonstration of Beijing's support for Kim Jong-Il as the next leader of Pyongyang.

Suddenly by the end of March, Beijing announced that Pyongyang informed them that Kim Il-Song will not visit the PRC until after the current crisis is resolved. High level Chinese sources suggested that Kim Il-Song is anticipating an imminent war and is therefore determined to remain in North Korea so that he can assume personal command over the liberation of the South. Furthermore, Beijing is somewhat relieved by the postponement of the visist because as long as the current nuclear crisis has not been resolved, a visit of this level would entail Western pressure on the PRC to impose a compromise on the DPRK, a compromise that both countries are determined to avoid.

Meanwhile, Deng Xiaoping has already issued in late January 1994 a directive ordering Beijing to "fully support" the DPRK in its hour of trial and difficulty. Originally issued in anticipation of the preparations for Kim Il-Song's forthcoming visit to Beijing, this Deng Xiaoping directive now constitutes the cornerstone of Beijing's policy toward the rapidly escalating crisis in Korea.

As the crisis mounts, Pyongyang's confidence in Beijing's strong support is fully justified. On 22 March, Premier Li Peng reaffirmed Beijing's opposition to applying pressure on North Korea. He warned that sanctions or other measures would inflame tensions further. Speaking in Beijing, Li implied that China would use its veto power at the United Nations Security Council to block any such moves. "China does not stand for pressure," Li said. "If pressure is applied, that can only complicate the situation on the Korean peninsula and add to the tension there."

Little wonder that North Korea is confident of China's support in its row with the world over nuclear inspections. Chu Chang-Jun, the North Korean ambassador to the PRC, said, on 23 March, that the Chinese President Jiang Zemin had personally assured Pyongyang of Beijing's friendship in the face of mounting fears that the current crisis might escalate into open confrontation. "Comrade Jiang Zemin said that no matter what changes take place in the universe, the friendship between China and the Democratic People's Republic of Korea will remain unchanged," ambassador Chu declared. A very assertive Chu then warned the US and its allies that "they have chosen the road which can lead only to war." He warned that "The American side should not forget the historical experience from the Korean War of the 1950s and should use it as a lesson. ... If they [the US] don't give up all those activities, nothing can happen but war," Chu Chang-Jun concluded.

30

RACE TO THE WIRE

Nevertheless, Pyongyang is raising the level of tension, creating an eve-of-war crisis environment. By late March 1994, the DPRK was actively pushing the Korean peninsula toward war. On the 25th, Pyongyang issued "an emergency alert order" to its entire military system, putting the entire KPA on high alert. Most noteworthy, the 650,000-strong KPA forces that were deployed along a 100-mile belt north of the DMZ were put on special alert. Also the training of KPA troops intensified all over the country. The DPRK is undertaking other measures as well. Among these measures are the examination of both the KPA's and the national emergency communication lines, the intensification of military training, and the increase of air defense facilities, the deployment and dispersement of assets, as well as increasing readiness of the entire Air Force and Air Defense system. Soon afterwards, the High Command informed the KPA that the wartime system has been activated. Consequently, the national mobilization system was activated to such a degree, that some 5 million reservists can now be mobilized within 12 hours. All these signs point to last minute preparations for war.

There are other signs that Pyongyang is advancing toward war. As of late March, the DPRK's propaganda machine began telling the entire population that "war appears inevitable." The North Korean TV and radio stations repeatedly broadcast that in view of the implacably hostile behavior of the Western-dominated IAEA, the country was determined to pull out of the NPT even though the risk would be grave for war with the US. Concrete steps are being taken to implement the decision to withstand the threat of war. A Chinese businessman who had just arrived from Pyongyang reported that it "had ordered its citizens to prepare for war." He described several measures taken in Pyongyang and throughout the DPRK—"maps showing key South Korean targets had been distributed among North Koreans" so that the citizens can follow the impending progress of the war of liberation. More ominously, the North Korean authorities have already imposed a 10-hour blackout and an overnight curfew throughout the country. The Chinese businessman also reported that massive civil-defense drills were being conducted repeatedly in Pyongyang.

Meanwhile, Pyongyang continues to raise the level of threats, warning that any sanctions imposed by the UN would be regarded as a "declaration of war." Starting 26 March, the North Korean threats have become increasingly specific. Pyongyang warns that the policy pursued by the US and its allies is already pushing the Korean peninsula toward war rapidly and irreversibly. "These provocative moves are very dangerous developments which may cause a catastrophic crisis on the Korean Peninsula," Pyongyang warns. As a direct outcome of Washington's declared policy, "a very grave situation fraught with the danger of war has been created on the Korean peninsula." Pyongyang stresses the inherent danger in the deployment of US military reinforcements and equipment to the region. "The United States had better look squarely at the seriousness of the present situation and ponder it over and must stop the reckless row of pressure and adventurous war moves at once." Later that day, the DPRK expanded the ultimatum to threatening Japan to stay out of the crisis. "If the situation on the Korean peninsula goes worse and a war breaks out, Japan will never be safe, either," Pyongyang warns. For the first time, the DPRK has raised the possibility of striking at Japan in a new Korean War. "The reckless military action of the Japanese reactionaries against the Korean people will result in digging their own grave." Taken together, these warnings and threats are aimed at ensuring that Washington, Seoul, and Tokyo fully realise the dire ramifications of challenging, let alone confronting, the DPRK.

In early April 1994, in his letter the conference of the WPK cell secretaries, Kim Il-Song emphasized the imminence and gravity of the crisis facing the DPRK. He stressed that a primary task now facing ther WPK cadres is to prepare the nation for mobilization and war. "Our struggle for socialist construction is waged in the accute confrontation with the enemies. Today, the imperialists and their stooges are intensifying the military threat and provocation maneuvers against our Republic, the fortress of socialism, with each passing day. The party cells should see to it that the party members and working people highten their revolutionary vigilence to cope with the enemy's aggressive provocation maneuvers, earnestly learn military affairs, and prepare themselves thoroughly in order to firmly defend the country's security and gains of socialism." Kim Il-Song then emphasized the growing importance of close and complete cooperation between the Army and the party cadres in this hour of trial for the DPRK.

Pyongyang sites Cambodia's King Norodom Sihanouk, an old friend of Kim Il-Song, as warning the West against the ramifications of aggression against the DPRK. "Today the danger of war is grave in the region and consequently in East Asia and the Far East, nay, in all our Asia. In this regard, the DPRK has committed no fault. It has only defended uncompromisingly its sacred right to complete independence in its own territory," Sihanouk declared upon arriving in Pyongyang on April 5th. The essence of this communique was to "demonstrate" to the North Korean population that their struggle enjoys the legitimization and support for world leaders.

April 5th, 1994, was a milestone in the North Korean war threats. An alarmist Pyongyang warned that war was imminent and that the current situation in the Korean peninsula was more severe than that on the eve of the Korean War of 1950-53. "A touch-and-go situation is prevailing on the Korean peninsula in which a war may break out any moment." Pyongyang pointed out that that all the factors needed to spark another major war in the Korean peninsula are falling into place. It is noteworthy that according to the North Korean version of the Korean War, the KPA went on the attack in reaction to an imminent and innevitable American offensive. Thus, the DPRK's war was defensive even though its KPA was on the offensive from the very beginning.

The same logic and depiction of circumstances are now being used by Pyongyang to describe the situation in the Korean peninsula. On 5 April, the DPRK argued that the US had already activated a contingency plan for an "attack" on the North. "The US military has worked out an operational plan to hurl 600,000 troops, more than 200 warships and 1,600 aircraft and so on from the US mainland within 80 days in case of an 'emergency' on the Korean peninsula," Pyongyang explains. "On bellicose orders from the US ruling quarters and under their aggressive war plan, 48 US missile launchers and a ... Patriot missile unit are on their way to South Korea at present. Overseas-based warplanes of various types are flying into US Air Force bases in South Korea one on the heels of the other, and the airlifted aggressor troops and lethal equipment are being deployed in operational zones. And US vessels including a nuclear aircraft carrier are at so close a range that they can reach the coastal area of Korea within 24 hours."

Pyongyang concluded that these and comparable "facts tell that the situation on the Korean Peninsula resembles that on the eve of the past Korean War." In a subsequent communique that day, the DPRK strongly implied that it may consider the deployment of the Patriot missiles as a justification for unleashing a preemptive war. "If the US and South Korean bellicose quarters brought Patriot missiles into South Korea and persistently sought a war in spite of the strong opposition of people at home and abroad, they would have to pay dearly for it," Pyongyang warns. There should be no doubt that the DPRK means war, and that its ready to fight the moment Kim Il-Song and Kim Jong-Il order the unification by force.

As anticipated, the spring session of the North Korean Supreme People's Assembly, held between 6 and 8 April 1994, was momentous in its revelations of Pyongyang's view of the escalating crisis. Both Kim Il-Song and Kim Jong-Il personally attended the opening session and, in his opening speech, Kim Il-Song warned that the DPRK was heading toward a fateful crisis. He urged an all-out effort and sacrifice to withstand it.

Indeed, the next day, the Assembly decided to increase defense spending. Finance Minister Yun Gi-Jong, loyal to Kim Jong-Il, declared that additional cash is being transferred to the military "to consolidate the defense capacity of the nation in face of the enemy's war provocation moves." He also warned that war was imminent, but added that "today our military potential has become mighty enough to drive back any provocation and surprise attack of the enemy."

Pyongyang's anticipation of an imminent war was clarified on April 8th in another major speech, this time by the KPA Chief of the General Staff, Vice Marshal Choe Kwang, who for the last couple of years has spoken with great authority on the DPRK's military strategy and intentions. His bellicose speech stressed that Korea is on the brink of war and that the KPA is ready for it. "The tense situation in which a war may break out at any time has been created in our country owing to the vicious anti-socialist, anti-DPRK campaigns of the imperialists and other international reactionary forces," Choe Kwang declared. "It is our unshakable will and policy to answer strength with strength, and dialogue with dialogue," he explained. "No machinations of the enemy can frighten our people and the People's Army that are under the outstanding leadership of a great brilliant commander [Kim Jong-Il]. ... If the enemy dare ignite a war, our people and the People's Army, unshakably determined to share the destiny with the party, will meet them courageously and wipe out the enemy relentlessly."

Choe Kwang emphasized the importance of Kim Jong-Il's leadership during the current crisis, leaving the impression that Kim Jong-Il was already the leader of North Korea. "With an outstanding and tested commanding art, [Kim Jong-Il] has wisely led the whole party, the entire people and the whole army to implement our party's line of self-reliant defense so that the defense capabilities of the nation have been consolidated rock-firm in all spheres. Today our People's Army has grown in strength and developed into invincible revolutionary armed forces with all services and arms, powerful means of strike and defense and unique tactics of *Juche*, which are sufficient for any modern warfare," Vice Marshal Choe Kwang concluded.

By now, the succession process in Pyongyang may be complete, with Kim Jong-Il the absolute leader of the DPRK. According to Ho Chong-Man, the Vice-Chairman of the Japanese *Chongyon*, the succession question has just been resolved. Returning from Pyongyang on April 5, Ho Chong-Man stated that "DPRK President Kim Il-Song has delegated full power — political, economic, and military — to the Workers' Party of Korea Secretary Kin Jong-Il." Ho Chong-Man is personally close to Kim Jong-Il and is considered a most knowledgeable source. At this time, there is no independent confirmation of Ho Chong-

Man's statement. It is note worthy that back in late March 1994, Kim Jong-II was expected to finally assume full powers during the spring session of the North Korean Supreme People's assembly. held between 6 and 8 April 1994. However. although Kim Jong-Il's leadership qualities were hailed during this session, the proceedings did not include a specific mention of such a transfer of power. Therefore, in the absence of an overt transfer of supreme power from Kim Il-Song to Kim Jong-II, the succession crisis in Pyongyang will continue to be a primary factor behind the growing instability and militancy of the DPRK.

It is evident now, more so than ever, that North Korea speaks with one voice. Its clear and belligerent tone can no longer be ignored or misinterpreted by those who, in the past, have given the DPRK a conciliatory benefit of the doubt.

Conclusion

Confronted with such global crises as the current situation triggered by North Korea, governments tend to seek a quick fix around the larger root causes. Washington is examining economic sanctions and surgical aerial strikes as two easy solutions for the time being. These steps, however, will be tough to execute. The odds against them working are even tougher. The DPRK is already isolated and bankrupt, so there is little more sanctions can achieve—especially since the PRC, Iran and other allies of Pyongyang refuse to cooperate.

Not only are surgical strikes are very difficult, but their ultimate success lies in much more then the ability of a certain number of aircraft to hit their targets. The main overriding questions are: Does the US have all the relevant intelligence on North Korean nuclear facilities? Should they choose to launch a surgical aerial strike, they must completely neutralize the DPRK's nuclear capabilities. There will be no second chances. The legacy of Iraq, then an IAEA member with an unblemished record of inspections, demonstrates that the IAEA can easily be fooled. It became clear after the Gulf War that US intelligence had grossly underestimated the scope of the Iraqi nuclear program and completely missed a host of extremely important sites. Major improvements in intelligence system have taken place in since the Gulf Crisis experience, but, nobody can be absolutely certain that Washington knows it all.

There should be no doubt the North Koreans will react with fury to any surgical strike, launching a general war against the South, using chemical and biological weapons. Are Seoul and Washington ready for that war? Is the inevitable and ensuing immense destruction in South Korea worth an attempt to neutralize the DPRK's nuclear capabilities? Are there options for dealing with the possibility of even a single nuclear device surviving such a strike? President Clinton threatened an all out nuclear strike on North Korea if it used the bomb. "It would be the end of their country," he stated during his visit to South Korea. But what will the United States actually do in case of a North Korean nuclear threat? How will Washington react to a threat from Beijing to stay out of a war in Korea or the PRC will also join the fighting just like in the 1950s?

Faced with these grim alternatives, the US and ROK can of course launch a war on the DPRK, effecting a unification by force of their own. But what will happen if the North Koreans use nuclear weapons in a desperate defense of Pyongyang? Will the US retaliate in kind against the soon-to-be-liberated citizens of an expanded ROK? How will Beijing take the entire spectre of a US-led offensive on one of its closest strategic allies just across the Chinese border? Will Russia tolerate such a drastic change in the regional strategic posture? What will be the impact of such a war on Japan, who now leads the world in economic appeasement of the DPRK? Will Japan take its revenge against the US through economic means? Considering all of these strategic and political ramifications, the initiation of a preemptive war is a highly unlikely move.

Thus, the US currently appeases North Korea. Washington is buying time and pretending that the DPRK does not have nuclear weapons. The US and its allies have settled into "do-nothing-for-now mode," attempting to appease Pyongyang through economic bribery and the IAEA inspection compromise. Meanwhile, Washington is getting used to the fact, though without acknowledging it to the American people, that the threat of North Korean nuclear blackmail is already hanging over our heads. It is hoped that time will deliver a mutually acceptable solution that Washington, Beijing, Tokyo, and even Seoul and Pyongyang, can live with.

But this is not likely to happen. Indeed, in his testimony in late January 1994 in front of the US Senate Intelligence Committee, DIA Director, Lt.Gen. James R. Clapper, USAF, stressed that North Korea "will remain the most critical major military threat to the United States through the middle part of the 1990s." Even if a new Korean War were not imminent, "the North continues to plan for a military option," Clapper said. In the meantime, the North Korean threat will only continue to rise simply because by the mid-to-late 1990s the DPRK would have perfected the nuclear-tipped *NoDong-X* ICBM that is capable of reaching the continental US. This fact alone will introduce a whole new dimension to the crisis in Korea.

Moreover, the tension building inside the DPRK is too great to contain. Only a dramatic breakout of the current decay can save Pyongyang from collapse. And the military is the only effective instrument available to them. Furthermore, the DPRK still considers itself committed to the joint grand design with the Iran led Islamic Bloc which calls for a simultaneous assault on America's allies and vital interests in the Korean Peninsula and the Middle East. Thus, Pyongyang has in effect two viable options: to attempt a regional nuclear extortion, demanding that Japan and ROK rebuild its economy, or to launch an all out effort for the sacred unification by force. Currently, these are the only viable options available according to Pyongyang. Hence, the looming spectre of the new Korean War, with its nuclear component.

And so, we live on borrowed time.

ABREVIATIONS

DMZ — DeMilitarized Zone (between North and South Korea)

CPC — Chinese Communist Party

DPRK — Democratic People's Republic of Korea (North Korea)

IAEA — International Atomic Energy Agency

ICBM — Inter-Continental Ballistic Missile

IRBM — Intermediate Range Ballistic Missile

KPA — (North) Korean People's Army

MBRL — Multiple Barrel Rocket Launcher

MIRV — Multiple Independently-targetted Reentry Vehicles (nuclear warheads)

MRBM — Medium Range Ballistic Missile

MRV — Multiple Reentry Vehicles (nuclear warheads)

NPT — Non-Proliferation Treaty

PRC — People's Republic of China

ROK — Republic of Korea (South Korea)

SAM — Surface to Air Missile

SSM — Surface to Surface Missile

TEL — Transporter, Erector, Launcher (of ballistic missiles)

WPK — Workers' Party of Korea

A NOTE ON SOURCES

With the Democratic People's Republic of Korea being the closest country on the face of the earth, obtaining detailed and authoritative material about its innermost secrets — such as the power struggle at the top and the extent of the military build-up — is not easy. Yet, as *Crisis in Korea* demonstrates, it is possible.

Crisis in Korea is based for the most part on extensive indigenous material from North Korea itself, as well as South Korea, Japan, the People's Republic of China, Russia (the USSR beforehand), and Iran. This material includes wire-service reports by local and international news agencies; numerous articles from the local news papers, periodicals, and newsletters; transcripts of broadcasts on the local media (mostly translated by the US Government's FBIS/JPRS), as well as a private collection of several thousand books, manuals and articles. In addition, the author draws on a unique private collection of primary sources developed over nearly two decades of intensive research. These include extensive interviews and communications with numerous emigres, defectors and otherwise involved individuals, plus original publications, documents and reports. This wide range of sources constitutes a unique data base for expert analysis regarding the subjects in question.

SELECTED BIBLIOGRAPHY

These are the primary sources used for the writing of *Crisis in Korea*. They constitute but a fraction of the diverse material consulted over the years of research.

NEWS AGENCIES

AFP (FRANCE)

AP (US)

INTERFAX (RUSSIA)

IRNA (IRAN)

KCNA (NORTH KOREA)

KYODO (JAPAN)

REUTERS (US/UK)

TASS (USSR)

XINHUA (PRC)

YONHAP (SOUTH KOREA)

MAIN PERIODICALS AND NEWSPAPERS

Asahi Shimbun (Japan)

Aziya i Afrika Segodnya (USSR)

Choson Ilbo (ROK)

Chungang Ilbo (ROK)

Daily Telegraph (UK)

Defense & Foreign Affairs: Strategic Policy (UK/US)

Defense & Foreign Affairs Weekly (UK/US)

Early Warning (US)

Economist (UK)

Far Eastern Economic Review (Hong Kong)

Foreign Report (UK)

Gunji Kenkyu (Japan)

Hoguk (ROK)

JANE's Defence Weekly (UK)

JANE's Intelligence Review (formerly *JANE's Soviet Intelligence Review*) (UK)

Jiefangjun Bao (PRC)

Krasnaya Zvezda (Russia/USSR)

Kulloja (DPRK)

Military Technology (Germany)

New York Times (US)

Nezavisimaya Gazeta (Russia/USSR)

Nodong Sinmun (DPRK)

Nodong Chongyon (DPRK)

Problemy Dal'nego Vostoka (USSR)

Renmin Ribao (PRC)

Sankei Shimbun (Japan)

Seoul Sinmun (ROK)

Sindong A (ROK)

Times (UK)

U.S. News & World Report (US)

Voyenno Istoricheskiy Zhurnal (Russia/USSR)

Washington Post (US)

Washington Times (US)

Wolgan Choson (ROK)

Zarubezhnoye Voyennye Obozreniye (Russia/USSR)

SELECTED BOOKS

Babin A.I. (ed.), *The Armed Struggle of the Peoples of Asia for Freedom and Independence*, Moscow, Nauka, 1984 [R]

Bermudez J.S. Jr., *North Korean Special Forces*, London, JANE's, 1988

Bermudez J.S. Jr., *Terrorism: The North Korean Connection*, New York NY, Crane Russak, 1990

Blair C., *The Forgotten War*, New York, Times Books, 1987

Bodansky Y., *Rogue Nukes*, New York, SPI Books, 1994

Bol'shov I.G. & Toloraya G.D., *The People's Democratic Republic of Korea*, Moscow, Mysl', 1987 [R]

Copley G.R. (ed.), *Defense & Foreign Affairs Handbook*, London, International Media Corp., several editions

George A.L., *The Chinese Communist Army in Action*, New York NY, Columbia University Press, 1967

Halliday J. & Cumings B., *Korea: The Unknown War*, New York NY, Pantheon Books, 1988

Ivanov A.I. (ed.), *Japanese Armed Forces*, Moscow, Nauka, 1985 [R]

Kim Hyun Hee, *The Tears of My Soul*, New York NY, William Morrow, 1993

Kirkbride Maj. W.A., *DMZ: A Story of the Panmunjom Axe Murder*, Elizabeth NJ & Seoul, Hollym International Corp., 1984

Kir'yan M.M. (ed.), *Geography of Militarism*, Moscow, Mysl', 1984 [R]

Kudasov S. & Moiseyev V., *The 38th Parallel*, Moscow, Novosti, 1988

Pacific Ocean Security, Moscow, Nauka, 1987 [R]

Park Jae Kyu & Ha J.M. (eds.), *The Soviet Union and East Asia in the 1980s*, Seoul, The Institute for Far Eastern Studies, 1983

Park Jae Kyu, Koh Byung Chul, & Kwak Tae-Hwan (eds.), *The Foreign Relations of North Korea: New Perspectives*, Seoul, Kyungnam University Press, 1987

Rees D., *A Short History of Korea*, New York NY, Hipocrene Books, 1988

Rhee Sang-Woo, *Security and Unification of Korea*, Seoul, Sogang University, 1984

Sandusky M.C., *America's Parallel*, Alexandria VA, Old Dominion Press, 1983

Shavrov Gen.Arm. I.Ye., *Local Wars: History and Present Day*, Moscow, Voyenizdat, 1981 [R]

Solomon R.H. & Kosaka Masataka (eds.), *The Soviet Far East Military Buildup*, Dover MA, Auburn House, 1986

Spurr R., *Enter the Dragon: China's Undeclared War Against the U.S. in Korea, 1950-51*, New York NY, Newmarket Press, 1988

Strategic Implications of the Soviet-North Korean Alliance, Proceeding of an International Security Council Conference, Seoul, Korea, 18-20 January 1987

Suh Dae-Sook, *Kim Il-Sung: The North Korean Leader*, New York NY, Columbia University Press, 1988

Summers H.G. Jr., *Korean War Almanac*, New York NY, Facts on File, 1990

The Soviet Union and the Security of East Asia, Proceeding of an International Security Council Conference, Seoul, Korea, 21-25 May 1985

Trigubenko M.Ye. (ed.), *The People's Democratic Republic of Korea*, Moscow, Nauka, 1985 [R]

[R] = Book in Russian